Sunless Freak

Sunless Freak

Memories of a Schizo

by

David Makepeace

About the Author

David is an over-30 skateboarder who enjoys a good nature walk where he resides in the Finger Lakes Region of New York State. He works as public speaker in the area of suicide prevention for NAMI Rochester. David also transports inter-library loan books for several local counties. As he says, to raise the Fahrenheit of dissent and deliver others due pleasure. You can usually find David taking a class at Writers and Books literary center, working toward his dream degree in Math & Physics, or improving at freestyle rap at the park 'n ride. David has been active in psychotherapy 15 years. Sober for 12 years. His message is helping others see recovery is possible so they can start to believe in their own recovery; just like people before David, they shared their stories to help him believe.

For privacy reasons, some names may have been changed.

For more information on Schizoaffective Disorder:
NAMI (National Alliance on Mental Illness)
If you are in a crisis, you're strong and you're needed. Today fucking sucks… but with help, tomorrow might not. Only one way to find out… be there. 1-800-273-TALK or visit Crisis Text Line. Don't be afraid to use this service. I was a crisis counselor on CTL. The people/counselors are dope people. They are ready to compassionately help you through today. There's no reason, no reason, you can't get help **right now.**

Dedicated to the skateboarding of Chris Cole.

Contents

Youth

I'm in bed and have a new feeling. It is a physical pain, but what we call human spirit is drubbed by depression.

I am a young, active and vigorous 14 year old.

I twist in the sheets.

I have no idea I have a mental illness. If you were to name it then whatever it is, it has allure.

Depression seduces with the pain. The pain I feel, it's now the expression of myself. I let this emptiness be my way of communicating.

I fling the sheet off me. It's a way I didn't know I could feel. I want to feel this way. I want to cut off others, isolate from the world.

I can't get out of the bed. I want no part in this new feeling. Something I don't want to feel. Hammers menace me here, a dangerous place. I don't like it.

I don't have to participate in the world. And the twisted allure of pain is sickening and pleasant.

I am coagulated like the coarse sand and chewed up gum from sandals in grout crevices on this ceramic tile I now look down at.

This is Spain. 19 years ago.

I continue to lie in bed after having caused confusion, worry and shock in my mother.

I still see through those shutter windows my family walking off to dinner. It was only after a fight to get me to go. I didn't answer her. Mom was exasperated by repeating to me, "What's wrong!?" Finally she gave up.

Home

My face is covered in acne. My skin is dry and it flakes. The pores of my nose are big and black-headed. I'm so self-conscious about all this. Someone said about my nose, "It's disgusting." I just never forgot that.

I scrub my face. Over and over with the soap. As if soap will cleanse away the now reddening, speckled face. Each night I return to my reflection.

(Looking in the mirror)

It didn't change. It's never going to change…

Dammit, there's no way out of this. What's the point of going on.

The eyes in the mirror dejected and sad.

Each night when I study my face these same thoughts come into awareness. Each time I study my face I re-connect the permanence of hopelessness with my situation.

The summer in Spain the person in the mirror looked about the same as the year before. I now feel different though. I can pin-point the exact moment hope gave out. In the hallway mirror of the Andalusian apartment, studying the zits on my shoulder in my reflection. I broke right there.

The usual reaction to my skin was to feel disconcerted. I turned from the mirror this time and felt the weight of depression for the first time. The feeling of hopelessness inside you which stays, makes an unwelcome home in you.

Depression made body image issues worse. Back at school - at my desk my head nestled in my sleeves. Depression is the dull feeling of sedation, some reticulated python now swallowing me as it devours a grown deer. There was always a sense of relative happiness.

My ceiling of the capacity to feel positive emotions had just lowered. Depression lingered everywhere as I walked to my next class. Hallways were transport lanes to commute to the next unfulfilling juncture. Just so subtle and insidious and ever-present.

Age 14. Same trip. France.

I left the chateau without telling anybody and climbed a quarter-ways up a mountain. There I sat. Alone. The grass in the wind soothed and called me to the beauty of melancholy. At that time I was exploring the feeling of depression. That need to be soothed was not something I encountered with meaning before. In other words, the experience of melancholic beauty. One hour on the mountain face. Serenity of dusk got me to flow with the feeling of unrest and I knew that being alone was beautiful and desirable. The lesson with me as I type.

My life began to come undone with youth infused with depression.

I became disinterested with school and fell from perfect student. I almost quit trying. I dropped or failed out of honors courses. Quit as captain of Academic Challenge Bowl. I was forced to play sports by my parents. If you're from a small-town you know that star athletes don't quit.

If you can imagine, a year previous I was the kid everyone thought had it together. I grew up hearing that from peers. I sat in the first row, looked to help any student, took to conversing with anyone socially excluded. The truth was, I thought I had no friends. It was by complete surprise then in Middle School I received the classroom Student Choice Award - consecutive years. The award won through student vote. Walking the hallways feeling like I didn't belong anywhere - then an hour later I'm chosen for a peer mediation training. I was chosen vice-president of student council. These things didn't matter. The truth is no matter how good it looks on the outside or what people are saying about you, anyone can have poor mental health.

It slipped past my parents when I dropped academic extracurriculars. They asked, but I answered I'd just lost interest. However, for myself, the changes at age 15 were not without repercussions. Feeling tired and fighting an uphill battle, I struggled in all academic courses that made me insecure.

In high school we were not taught basic psychology terms related to mental health. It is only in retrospect that I can see how my self-esteem was damaged as a kid, and that this negative sense of self was reinforced by depression.

"Head up," that old refrain.

The python closes its mouth and retracts down into the wooding and below the classroom-floor. It hisses when my eyelids get heavy.

My eyes refocus on the chalkboard with no knowledge of where in the lesson we are. I've missed 20 minutes of instruction. I try to keep my head upright and use muscles to stay alert. Nothing comprehensible comes out of the last 15 minutes. Once in a while Mrs. Proul takes me aside after class to discuss my grades and inattention during class.

I can't do the work because I have no idea where in the course we are, or what we've been taught so far. This failure becomes something I just blame on my own stupidity.

The level of disengagement during school made it feel like being in a waiting room for no reason. The walls of slogans such as, "Life Is Good!" began to feel like mini-malls of generic advice sold on t-shirts that charge extra because enough people want to buy them.

Still I struggled to find intellectual satisfaction somewhere, with depression always somewhere in the background and the hopelessness

By age 15, I still was questioning what my friendships amounted to. Did I even have friends? There came a period of extended questioning. After which, I gave up seeking to engage much with others.

I hit play on the song Orbital - "Halcyon + On + On."
My forehead I place on the computer table.
15 minutes go by.
My mix has made it to Radiohead, "Karma Police."

"Why do I have this life?" I think.

"Why can't I be free — on my own? Away from all this?"

I feel so melancholy I lift my eyes to the computer. The file folders are fuzzy and screen light glows.

"It's not done yet? This is my last episode."

6 episodes later, it's 4 AM.

I carry my body to the corner of the basement and fall in a heap. School's in a few hours.

"I'm cutting out early tomorrow. I don't care."
I feel heavy and hopeless.

My eyes shut like a computer screen where the world of fantasy has afforded me a night of escape. Like the phenom mic controller song of that year by Eminem, played in every afterschool parking lot or varsity basketball warm-up:
"Snap back to reality/
Oh, there goes gravity."

In space there's no friction. An object will continue at the same speed uninterrupted unless struck by another object or pulled in by the gravitational force of another planet.

Head lifts from pillow.
Body dragged upstairs.
Another day…
In the gravitational pull
Of this planet
In small town orbit.

The Internet was taking hold by 2003. In my searches for new music I discovered Stanton Message Boards, a forum with members devoted to the different elements of DJ'ing. Washing dishes and with a little financial help from my kid brother I purchased a turntable set-up. My mother even went and bought me Doug Pray's documentary *Scratch*. To this day an all-time classic in telling the story of Hip Hop. I began learning to beat-match, scratch, beat-juggle and mix. Stanton's community supported and inspired me to pursue my means of self-expression.

What school became was hands on a clock that had to get to a certain arrangement. When

2:45 hit I booked it. I would go underground into the basement to my turntables and music production software to immerse myself back into the subculture.

The need to participate in school and its importance was over. I knew where the pool doors were for a back exit. Now on bad days I just left and ate a detention the next week.

My parents were noticing things. It caused a lot of anxiety for them to watch me isolate. They couldn't tell if something was wrong or if puberty and the changes kids undergo was afoot. The subculture was exciting and fulfilling so I never considered what was wrong with the behavior of isolation. I didn't even know art was my sanctuary from a difficult and indifferent world. I just did it because it felt right.

A lot of people fascinated with drugs and alcohol, I don't believe found many healthy outlets for their uncomfortable feelings. Granted, I still played sports, my parents wouldn't budge on that. I would prefer to write a poem rather than waste a night sitting around a table like zombies snorting Oxies. Didn't appeal to me. I liked weed and booze but it never did much.

I used to watch a table of girls. Their names were Shawna and Rachel. Shawna was a model kid, the toast of Livonia. Then she somehow got involved in heroin along with a crew of others. One day walking my usual route home I saw her ahead of me. She reached out her hand to touch the evergreen tree and brushed it through the needles. I saw her do that and felt that twinge of beauty and such desire. When you see something beautiful, especially done by a beautiful person, it comes with the perception there's hurt touching something in a malaise of incomprehension of the world. Or a small-town world. An addiction. A wonder, a curiosity. Something en-raveled in what's also sick. Something to touch. I felt desire to be near her, because in that moment I knew there was something happening that I identified with. From that moment on when I passed that same tree I reached out and brushed my hand through the needles.

School was no longer keeping me intellectually stimulated. Learning music production software became my focus. I re-inspired myself, getting my kicks from learning what I wanted to learn. In a way, I tried harder. That was very healthy, but I repeat, the healthy outlets for my pain involved excessive isolation.

In a great way, though certainly not re-assuring to them, my parents gave me space and thus helped my learning flow freely. Their protestations about my isolation were constant, but they never intruded farther to stop me.

In regard to isolation I think that's a lot of kids. I imagine, through my own experience, reasons exist very natural to behave like that. Nowadays, the classes I teach we point out to students isolation as a behavior in a list of warning signs. Isolation isn't the sign of mental illness. It's simply common to people with mental illness. At this very moment I hope not to betray the confidence of this reader saying any less than: isolation should never be demonized. Isolation is a natural direction and important to the development of independent thinking.

Back in 2003, we're operating where the invisible illness meets a society that does not popularize or shed light on mental illness.

You may now understand the difficulty my parents faced. Not knowing anything about my grandfather, the true meaning of words we say everyday now like Anxiety, Depression, Bi-Polar Disorder were in the dark. And still, they allowed me space to learn and cope, and they got me professional help. That's as well done as it gets. And simply put, for the rest, it's no one's fault.

Without basic knowledge like what is mental health? Do we all have mental health? How do we keep our mental health feelin' good? We're all sort of blind out here.

I coined this phrase. Or rather, I discovered it after lost hiking without a map in the Tuscarora Forest outside Carlisle, PA. (where I attended Dickinson College). You don't have the critical information, then you know nothing.

"Without intelligence, you have no intelligence."

I made it back to civilization, after a few tense hours.

And New York State just mandated mental health education for every school.

Hooray for our team!

What taught me how to think was not school. Art taught me how to think. Independent thought brought me confidence. I know what I appreciate now. Art and freedom. I live for the 87% grade and making any excuse to go to the art room with my buddy Dan.

By age 17, with a newfound love for art and self-expression, things got better. I got a girlfriend and lost my virginity. My skin issues came to be less of a nuisance. There wasn't a feeling like I didn't belong somewhere.

I went to reggae concerts. I danced at parties. I had a skateboarding crew. It began to feel like I had a normal life.

Still a day after school spent alone making beats was preferable to socializing. The days of being able to isolate were becoming less and less though. People began to invade the basement to pull me off the MIDI keyboard. Maybe because I was a turntablist and musician people thought I was cool. That didn't matter much. Wasn't why I spun or made beats. It never hurts to feel your company is desired by peers. Especially when you've suffered alone in silence.

In my senior year there was a sense of kinship among people and I didn't mind partying on the weekends or getting into mischief. I still needed nights to skateboard alone.

I close the door softly. The night is cool and my hoodie feels heavy and secure. The board cracks that pavement when I reach the driveway's end. On my iPod I select melancholy electronic music like Orbital, or my favorite album DJ Shadow's *Endtroducing*.

My swansong to Livonia was buying 25 cans of spray paint and getting 3 friends to join in writing NYC subway style graffiti all over our town and high school. The words Brad wrote were haunting. In dripping letters, "Time Heals Us."

I was arrested in my home.

The graffiti and my arrest led to public humiliation for the family. I was sentenced to 90 days intermittent incarceration served on a weekend prison crew, 3 years of probation. Given therapy as a non-negotiable parental request.

The therapist asks, "So, David, let me start by asking. How are you feeling?"

"I'm good."
I feel anxiety.

Right then, I realize there are massive things I need to release. In retrospect, 25 sessions worth of stuff pressing on my mind.

The therapist pauses.

"I say this to all the guys and girls who come here. This is a safe place for us to just have a discussion about what's been going on in your life. It's totally up to you to share or we can just talk about anything. There's no pressure. We can talk about whatever you'd like to talk about."

I feel paralyzed. How can I say these things? How do I know they're OK? What if I start and all this stuff comes out? It could really, really mess me up.

My head feels heavy as the anxiety grows and crushes me as it surfaces. I don't voice it.

I use a grown-up voice and talk about how well and fucking dandy life's going. Every line is hiding. Lies in every word because each sentence omits that I really need to be talking about something. And what is it? I have no idea; it's just a heavy feeling I have and something I can't volunteer or express in words.

I'm asked to draw how I feel as homework. At home I draw a face full of chaotic lines, frustration, congestion and pain.

Art taught me how to think. I got the B+ average.

Therapy lasted 3 sessions.

I needed to get far away. As far as in-state tuition allowed me.

I went to college.

Therapy Session .01

9 Years After High School

"You know, David. I just thought of something. You've been in therapy a long time haven't you? Would it be correct to say you start and stop therapy a lot?"

"Yes, that's true."

"Does it ever feel like you have one foot in and one foot out? Like it's hard for you to commit to therapy? What do you think about that?

"Yes. That's exactly how I feel."

"I think you might have a problem with intimacy, David."

My eyes widen.

I feel totally vulnerable. I feel hopeful.

"What do you think the reason is for that?"

"Because I'm afraid. I'm really afraid. I don't think I can be close to anyone."

"I'm sorry to hear that, David. That must be really tough."

I tear up.

"It is hard."

Long pause.

I feel crippled and helpless. I feel hopeful.

"David, I think we really hit on something."

"That's really my main issue. I really struggle with that. I want closeness and to feel something. I just don't know how."

"Why don't we do some homework on this? I want you this week to use your imagination and imagine what it would be like to be close to someone. If it gets to be too uncomfortable you can stop. Whatever practices you need to use if it gets to be too much, only do what you're comfortable with…but challenge yourself too, David."

"Yes. I think we really found the issue."

"Let's work on intimacy this week, OK."

"I'm ready for this. I think we identified something."

I'm thrilled. This is a breakthrough.

"Thank you, Jeanette."

College

It's possible to switch places and have temporary release from mental illness. You exist in a haze of newfound freedom, excitement, and joy. You are introduced to new people, and old troubles just vanish. Just, gone. It was the small-town orbit. It was those people, places and things. They must be the real source of discomfort.

I make friends easily. It's scary how fast and widely people want my company. Now, being largely symptom-free, well, there's this song. It sums up my personality:

"Gigantic. Gigantic.
A big big love."

As a freshman I'm placed into a philosophy mini-program. On the weekends I go to NYC and meet Jack's friends, graffiti artists and rappers from Boston. I partake on campus with an unofficial DIY frat called, "Party Train."

The excitement walking out of the dorm everyday greets me with a Marb Red at the plunk spot where all would wander in and out of each day making conversation. Constant state of devout thanksgiving for my new life of freedom from small-town peril, where places ate their own. No outlets for kids who hate school. Beefed up graffiti charges.

I spread seeds of friendship everywhere. Jack, my roommate. Miles. Bald Dave. And Jane, Sylvia and Cat. Dan, Conor. Ian.

It's mid-freshman year and friendships blossoms with nothing to rag on. No depression. No anxiety. No isolation.

It was a constant dream worn on my face, like winter's end and the smiling face of spring.
Purchase is an art school parading as a liberal arts school. Its students are all artists, or

have majors outside art but are artistic. There are concerts almost every night at the Stood which is a student center complete with arcade games, skateboarding ramps, and a stage. I watch Benevento/Russo Duo blow the top off the Stood, Skerik's Syncopated Taint Septet put together an astounding show that traveled out the venue with instruments around campus. Girl Talk played mash-ups, in the heyday of mash-ups, and accidentally mule kicked a woman in the 'noggin. Purchase rules are a little more relaxed. I enjoy the company of its students and the freedoms like buying smokes at the campus store or chasing campus tours around covered in fake blood yelling out anti-war slogans. I have no idea if it's been changed, but our school slogan back then was, "Think Wide-Open."

Still as a freshman, 2 exchange students, Fabiola and Kim, become my first meaningful relationships with women based in platonic love.

"You're warm and beautiful Kim. I'm not letting go." I'm hugging Kim from behind her computer chair.

"Nope."

Kim laughs.

"Kim, if you want, I will. Wait a second, ah, no way you're too warm. She's a great dancer. Right Fab?"

Fab lets out a sarcastic chuckle.

"She did amazing. You're awesome Kim. What are you doing on your computer I'm here. It's so nice here. I'll let go?"

"No don't," Kim says smiling.

We slip into bed, us 3, and watch movies, and I can never stop hugging or being affectionate with them. Coming from an international family of Spanish teachers I get along with foreigners well. Fabiola and Kim, I grow to love and in spending time with them begin to love women in a mature respectability.

Jane took my hand and drew a big black heart on the web between the thumb and pointer. I watched in silent awe. I felt so elated. It seemed love was something I was worthy of and I felt nervous about people expressing love toward me, but also surrendering to why not give this a shot.

There's a mood-altering element to college. It's this exuberant feeling in you of what's next? What could possibly happen next? I cannot wait to see it. There's this sense in me at least, profound love for everything. The joy of seeing someone I know or am getting to know! I want to talk to them. I want to see about hanging out.

Every time I turned around I'd see someone smiling. Someone happy to see me. I was at last, very popular.

Looking back, freshman and part of sophomore year is when time stands still. But things change. You can't hide from your past like every vocalist sallies another pop loop with. And with mental illness it's the tiger that's been stalking the grounds just off-campus. It seems some days I come to the plunk spot alone and see a flash of him just beyond some dorms in the distance.

And then, it begins to bound toward you.

Sophomore Year

In spring of 2007, I fell in young love or infatuated with Sylvia and it ended hard. It had all the makings of first love syndrome; the feelings of longing were intolerable and by middle of sophomore year I ran away to New Orleans. I spent 5 days looking for work. Riding trolleys. I sat on my bunk-bed at the cheapest hostel in the French Quarter. I didn't feel any different. I decided to take the Greyhound back when I realized the verb, "to run".

The Day I Ran

It was a nice enough day at Purchase when I walked outside the dorm. I had on my backpack with a couple books. I headed to class, and then I saw her coming up the way. I made some kind of face I don't remember, maybe a scowl. A scowl for how she ditched me, or how things didn't work out, or all the shit, unhappiness, longing I don't remember. What I do remember was that day taking a turn away from the humanities building and deciding right then and there to run. I was formulating my plan as I went. I was to go to New Orleans and start over fresh. I would go to a place that sounded enticing, and had started romanticizing a place that was rebuilding, and a place where I too would build again.

And then a strange thing happened. As I was walking the circuitous route that runs around campus all of the sudden it started to rain. It was light at first and then began to hit me harder and harder. To my astonishment the sun which had been hidden that day suddenly emerged through a veil of cloud to create a bluish-white aura that came over me like cleansing fire. God knows what it was, probably just an odd coincidence, but given the timing I thought of it as very odd, and perhaps a sign. I was on the right track.

I hitchhiked to White Plains where I headed directly to the bus station. On my way I formulated that by going to Albany first to say my goodbyes to a good friend Conor, and getting some supplies as I had left campus with only my clothes and a couple books with no intention of going back, only then I would be on the road. I bought a ticket to Albany and met Conor at the station. He was fascinated by something, the random craziness, or suddenness of it all. To his credit he set me up with a leather jacket, sleeping bag, hat/mask, knife, and underwear. The next day I was gone.

There, New...Orleans

I walk the French Quarter, buy a po-boy, and continue to wander. I'm looking for the feeling of elation to cure my ills. Carry me away from the past. This prescription I wrote myself is nowhere in New Orleans. I can't find elation riding trolleys. I can't find it walking or applying for jobs at Subways or non-profits. It's missing in the thick humidity. In fact the sweat is always on my brow and feeling so desperate is so constant. I cannot feel grounded.

In an internet cafe I check messages. A deluge of emails and notifications perform in my eyes. I check a couple. A slow realization is taking place. Even if I take the name of a dead man, get a job, and get an apartment, the social context of my relations with friends and places cannot be severed. I realize that. Even now as I look outside this cafe at the passing of people,

I am a visitor here. Where else is calling me but the place that impulsive behavior led to escape from. One fact is the same. The same since early youth. But it never can reach me. I am hurt and require help.

Junior

It's junior year where my mental health begins to deteriorate. That haze of new freedom and all those soaring feelings of joy have deserted me. I walk around campus empty. School is like being stranded in limbo, the last one at a concert without a ride.

The feeling of limbo led to a decision to satisfy my need for fulfillment outside of Purchase College. For a couple months I would take the bus after my morning classes, volunteer for several hours at a non-profit, then catch the bus back to school. They were long days, but what carried me was that I was doing something *finally*. I began getting used to the dress-shirt and tie. The employees at the

Coalition were all down-to-earth. This felt like an opportunity.

I took a break from SUNY-Purchase before the start of second semester of junior year. The place where I'd been volunteering, The Westchester Hispanic Coalition, had an Office Manager position open up. The timing was impeccable. After a few weeks of proving myself at the central office in White Plains (I'm 20 at the time), I was given my own satellite office to do case-management for unpaid wage claims, file rental assistance applications, run a day-laborer site, and be a hub of support to Latinos in Port Chester, my beloved city.

I would go to the square at night and wail on that fucking harmonica. Man, I couldn't play a lick but I stretched those tones out!

I grew interested in politics. Obama was running. On Ave. of the Americas I went to conferences and did training with The National Day-Laborer Organizing Network in Phoenix. We protested Joe Arpaio in the streets.

"Down with the Sheriff, with the MEAN MEAN SHERIFF. UP with the people, up up with the people, up with the HOPES AND DREAMS OF THE PEOPLE…UP UP WITH THE PEOPLE AND down with the Sheriff." We chant for an hour. It feels amazing to be with strangers who share a common cause all connected as young people through the thread of NDLON.

I open the door to the meeting room. In the middle of the room are seated the 6 heads of NDLON. I can tell it's a private meeting, no matter.

"Hi, thought I'd come in and join you. I'd like to be a part of whatever the organization is discussing if you'll have me."

Slightly bewildered, "Sorry this is a private meeting," one woman says.

The Head of NDLON, Pablo Alvarado is grinning at me from ear to ear.

Pablo pulls me aside the day before we're scheduled to leave. He is not a loud man, unless he laughs. His words are decisive.

"I've noticed this week that the others have come to respect you. You have the makings of a leader. I'd like, if you accept the offer, to fly you to different sites across the US to meet affiliates of our organization and educate yourself on our operation."

I'm surprised.

"This is a very enticing offer. I would be very excited to say yes right now. I will think it over and get back to you ASAP."

"OK," Pablo says, and smiles.

Some days while walking the Port Chester streets I can focus on work matters. Other days, my mind feels so restless.

I pass Hubba's the big stewing pot of meat sauce sits in the front window. Salvation Army. The Brazilian BBQ joint. I'm hot, I'm edgy, ENOUGH.

Walking Main Street, I get a sensation of shattered glass in my skull with its edges rubbing and itchy. In the office I go to re-check yesterday's posts on music forums and they read loopy. I'm losing touch with reality but I have no awareness of the progression of the psychosis.

The most I knew about schizophrenia was someone might mention their aunt had it and basically dismiss them as a lunatic. To be fair, I hadn't really been taught what "mental health" even was.

The summer days are hot. I watch chess matches at night on the steps of elegant marble banks punctuated by a crotch-rocket of some hot-shot who might be my roommate I rarely see.

I was completely functional even while being undiagnosed and untreated for mental illness. My work rarely suffered from the effects of isolation and the disorder, but I had begun drinking alone really for the first time in my life. Drinking in college was something I did socially in moderation. Stuffed up in a tiny apartment in Port Chester, with only my turntables, computer, and a tiny TV that streamed CNN all day. I buy a 6-pack from the bodega and lie back if the debates are on.

At summer's end, in my office I would watch for the clock hands to get to a certain arrangement. 5 PM, lock the door, roll a joint, and go catch the latest movie at the AMC and crash.

I rarely see friends.

I take the bus from Westchester Ave @East Broadway, the bus-stop below the bread factory 33 minutes to Waller Ave in White Plains to the Non-Profit HQ for the last time.

I leave Port Chester.

The apartment above H&R Block on 30 S. Hanover Street, Carlisle, PA, 3 staircases and 229 miles…

229 miles SW.

Where would I be if I talked to somebody about what I was going through?

As I type within the light of a one-room apartment somewhere in time and space.

The early diagnosis.

The pre-emptive measures.

Can never reach me. I am hurt and require help.
I must go down the dark alley where change and loose screws get strangely dispersed. Down the corners of bars. All of a life, take all of a life. I will go to the place.

And I'm glad now, you're with me, because:

Sometimes it gets too quiet,

To inexperience this.

Carlisle, PA/
Psychosis Progression

I pack up the minivan.

Spring of junior year, I'd decided to attend Dickinson College for a private study with Crispin Sartwell. I had read a couple of Crispin's books, and to be frank was astounded by not only his theories which were interesting in their own right but by how cool it was. It was his voice, which was at times angry, but always challenging and it was about blowing up arguments and confessing the most gritty of life experiences with philosophy.

My father is an excellent man. He isn't like Crispin. My father is the best kind of man (but at 20 years old, and I don't know it) but I need a model to emulate how to be a strong fearless man. The kind of man my father is was never a model of that outwardly. My father is very dedicated, loving and extremely virtuous! He doesn't exhibit strength and power outwardly; it is always behind-the-scenes and thus I was not mature enough to understand how it was modeled to me.

In all honesty, at the time I had no idea why I gravitated to Crispin; except to point to the content and style of his writings and later my perceived shortcomings as a man.

Crispin warns me in an email about Carlisle, "It ain't exactly Paris."

I imagine that my friends at this point say stuff only in odd whispers: "Where did Dave go? Haven't seen him around. Heard he was in Gettysburg. Heard he went to study somewhere in Pennsylvania. He deleted his Facebook. I miss that Makepeace." I drank hard, isolated, squatted, worked at McDonald's, got paid to wear a Statue of Liberty suit, drove drunk, got kicked out of apartments, missed class, and cannot remember a laundromat.

My roommate Darren was a reformed neo-Nazi and a father. We played Bob Marley's *Greatest Hits* and smoked Pall Mall in the nicotine tinged walls as the yellow fever of drugs and isolation made me twitchy and crept under my fingernail skin like chemical stains. A stone's throw from the apartment was the Hammer-smiths tattoo shop. Demented freak demon firefighters with SS tattoos and red-dried eyeballs tattooed on the back of skinned heads at our apartment. I was burnt out after 2 months. I fell asleep on park benches and wailed the harmonica to Little Walter's "Blue Midnight." Stumbling over keys drunk in front of a laptop. Abandon it, go buy beer. Nothing was sane. Nothing was stable. Nothing in my life had routine and so the slip started until one night, alone and squatting, I returned from the bar and fell in the kitchen. I reached up to the counter-top a sick wounded animal moaning out of its misery and toppled back to the floor, only to awaken to the demented screams of vagrants on the shit-stained curbs of clinics with oxidized windows and empty looking offices.

I wrote Sylvia a postcard and she sent one back. Reading it only confused me: "When you're ready to stop hiding." The verb "to hide" is not far from the verb "to run."

At Dickinson I had no friends, stability, or knowledge of the fact that the progression of my psychosis was making it impossible to function as a normal human being. The resurgence of mental illness into my life from the end of my time at the Coalition till now, as it worsens I still have absolutely zero idea I have a mental illness.

I drank every night to mask and cope with this enigmatic feeling. Also, I began romanticizing alcohol and the philosopher-artist mentality. No wisdom is suspended in the glass.

Carlisle, the naively religious but always patriotic Miss Teen USA of all towns. I pass it heading south and still feel the sickening vibrations coming from the dense rotted steel heart, hemorrhaging another vagrant scream.

Senior

Senior year I'm back at Purchase. I feel a lot of sadness. In the shower I crumple to the floor gasping and in terror. The depression is back. I drink more. I alienate my friends. I've lost track of schoolwork.

By mid-senior year I'm drunk every night. There are a few campus apartments where a once welcome friend now just shows up with Budweiser 40's or 2 bottles of red on a Tuesday night. He drinks them down and is very lovable or can seem like a different person. There was a point I reached where I didn't study a lick and focused solely on my senior project when, that is, I focused on anything.

Jane and Cat supported me. I did damage to our friendship; those most important felt it. I got lost in my senior project, weed, and drinking. Wasting away in my private world where everyone watches on fearfully and Jane and Cat strain themselves to watch out for me.

In Economics class one day I felt panic set over me. I couldn't sit still, fight or flight, a need to run. I grab my books and bee-line out of the lecture hall. When I got outside I felt the panic lessen, but I was far from right. I knew there was a counseling center on campus and it made the most sense to go there, see someone, get some kind of relief.

I found the counseling center, waited patiently, raking some sand and trying to keep the panic minimized though it surged in waves. I sat down with a counselor after 45 minutes of dawdling and began.

I cannot recall the conversation, only the eyes that were wide with shock. She looked for no comprehension in my words, as I rambled through tens of issues (all I thought, related) as to why I was feeling this way. It was the babble of disorganized thinking from a psychotic state and her eyes, those startled, fearful eyes that I didn't understand. I was too far gone.

Finally she interrupted and said kindly I should go to the hospital just to be checked out. That it was standard procedure to be taken in an ambulance, just wait here, that help was on its way.

Befuddled. In my psychotic state I took it as normal procedure for transport and I waited for men to wheel me on a gurney, as students watched, into the back of the truck and take me away.

Later that night I saw a psychiatrist. I rambled for 20 minutes in what must have been a shocking display of psychotic dialogue. I vented from Dickinson College years to where I was sitting, non-stop for 20 minutes. Even I felt something rather odd about what I was saying. After I finished, he slid a piece of paper in front of me. He said to sign it and said it would be my ticket into the hospital for the night, and the next day I would be released. Well, I didn't have a car, and it was late. I signed the paper.

Little did I know I was now under the supervision and the restrictions of the mental health system. Boy was I ticked off. When I wasn't released the next day I made inquiries about the promise that was made. I asked about what they were doing with me, and how the fuck do I get out of here. After spending the day in a tizzy, I decided to write a letter about how I was being held against my will.

Names of Witnesses (Last Name) Makepeace (First Name) David (MI) B

Description Briefly; I arrived (1/25) @ St Vincent Hospital at about 1:30 PM, coming from Suny Purchase via ambulance, which is a standard protocol for any student who wants to see medical staff @ Vincent. The morning of (1/25) I met for first time the counselor who recommended seeing a psychiatrist here, reluctantly I chose to. At 5:00 I was seen by Dr. ███████. Afterward, (1/26) after spending the night @ Vincent I realized Dr. ███ was engaging in misconduct by falsely describing the circumstances of my voluntary admittance to the Ward. I admitted myself on the condition I would be discharged around 12:00 the next (1/26) day before my 2:30 PM college class, which Dr. ███ assured me would happen. I am currently being held against my will and understanding. The doctor staff has since both neglected to give grant me audience and is now indicating I must have further tests/examinations before being discharged. These excessive tests are not neccesary nor desired now. I have been briefly glossed over by one doctor to the next, lied to, and now imprisoned against my will. This is a disastrous climate for anyone who wished simply for a consultation a found themselves trapped at a vulnerable time.

Signature ~~~~ Date 1/26/10

Questions or comments: opmc@health.state.ny.us
Disclaimer Privacy Policy

When the supervisor of the ward got wind of it, she came into my room accompanied by 2 men with a glass of water and some pills. No way in hell was I taking those pills, I thought. They said that I had to or they would force me to take them. I had no idea how deep I was in. I argued a bunch about how I was promised to be freed, and how they were making me angry. Finally, under the pressure I broke down and took the pills. A strange sense of relief came over me after a couple hours; it seemed I was in a resting place.

Mom and Dad drove all the way from Upstate NY to visit me on day 3 at St. Vincent's. Their unconditional love would have taken them anywhere on the globe in 24 hours for their son. I was still in a tizzy over being held against my will, but the medication which I took begrudgingly had me sedated. I told my parents it was all some misunderstanding and explained to them enough that, with their assistance, I was released.

We said our goodbyes and I promised them things would be alright. Upon return to Purchase things didn't get better. I continued to reach for the bottle to drink and drug, to mask and cope with undiagnosed and untreated mental illness.

Sitting on a campus protective-ledge in winter. Luda stops to talk.

"Hey Dave."
"Hey."

Pause.

"Are you alright?" says Luda.

A hundred thoughts have been swirling.

I don't speak.

She stands there looking mistrustful.

"I'm fine."
"Are you sure?"

I don't speak.

"I'm fine."

No.

In 10 days…

I broke.

Winter/Psychotic Break

Winter of 2009 things reach a breaking point. I'm sitting on a bench down the street of our White Plains apartment crying and dripping with phlegm. I am distraught. I'm holding onto fragments with nowhere to turn.

"Who am I?"

There is a deep wide chasm you fall through if you dance down there too close to the edge–with yourself, who you are, and the falsehood of who you must be. I cried for an hour at the basketball court above our house. By the time all the phlegm had dried on my sleeve I went inside and crumpled into a heap in the corner of my room. I had taken my clothes off. The

Venetian shades scissored me in sections as my inflating chest pressed the lacquered wood floor. I'm nothing but a small spark left. I've got nothing, I don't know what else to say.

The Night it All Broke

Out of nowhere, the feeling like a lasso is squeezing your temples. The disorientation begins. I don't understand. I'm enlightened so why do I feel this enormous pain? I stumble out of the kitchen and down the stairs into the street.

I'm moaning and stumbling down the street. I'm feeling waviness and looseness in my head. I'm in terrible confusion and pain.

Suddenly the telephone post to my right changes to the color purple and it moves toward me. It's coming towards me. I panic.

I'm so disoriented I'm walking now down the hill towards the mini-mall on the rich side of Westchester. I can't remember what I'm saying. It's unintelligible grunting and moaning. The word, "Help," might have come out.

It's the wee hours of the morning. There's nothing I can do. I wheel around sensing at least that I need to return home and get some help. The only thing I'm cognizant of in this psychotic break is I need help. Not every person who is floridly psychotic can have that realization, but luckily I do.

By the time I get back to the apartment I again rouse Conor and tell him something really bad is happening to me. I tell him it's urgent and I have to go to the hospital NOW!

He's so dazed he doesn't understand. It takes him 5 minutes to get himself together and when he walks out of his room I'm sitting leaning on the wall of the kitchen hallway. I plead with him to help get me to the hospital. He says he'll help.

As I wait for him to call a cab suddenly my vision is changing. I'm a mixture of extreme panic and disorientation, but I feel my vision closing though my eyes are open. It's going black. It strikes me that this is it. I am about to die. This is the blackness that comes over in your last moments living. Then with my eyes wide open my vision goes out. It goes black.

Conor helps me up. I can see again. I rush to gather some things in my backpack, which is funny because even in a psychotic break I have a few realizations.

One thing: what's happened to me will take years to correct. Two: I'm going to need essential items for staying in the hospital for a long time, but I fail obviously in my state when Conor is alarmed that I'm trying to stuff a basketball into my book bag.

We get in the cab and luckily the hospital is 1.5 miles away. I'm terrified. Conor is tired. We arrive and I walk through the main doors with Conor by my side. As I enter I crash my hip into the service desk while moaning loudly.

It gets the attention of the staff immediately. Within 1 minute, bless these people, they have me in an examination room. A kind and very direct nurse begins asking me questions.

She asks, "David, what's the last thing you thought about?"

I answer, "The sleep of reason produces monsters."

She says, "You need to stop reading those fantasy books."

The humor is lost on me.

The nurse understands I am in dire need of a further examination. I am placed on a gurney and wheeled into a room with a big light above me. For a few minutes I'm totally alone. In those minutes I realize I am in restraints, but I'm so psychotic and scared that I accept them and don't protest.

A middle-aged man enters the room followed by 2 orderlies. He approaches me with a small flashlight and shines it right into my eye. He says, "Can you keep your eye open?" I comply.

Then asks, "Are you dreaming?"

I am unsure of what to say.

The doctors and orderlies leave and my mind is spinning. I remember my friend Eric Mendenhall's Facebook picture is of his back turned to the camera, him as a child. I glean some evidence in my daze that he and I have a childhood that is under watch. It dawns on me, these people, who've come into this room are members of the observational task force that has watched me my whole life. Eric is another case study and we are test subjects of some nature.

Yet as soon as I go into this delusion people enter and whisk me off somewhere else. That delusion will return however.

I am taken by 2 men who are in a good mood to get a scan of my brain. I teeter in and out of psychosis. As they're wheeling me I come to my senses and they make playful conversation with me. In retrospect, I don't know if they were humoring me but I seemed to have become sane again.

The scan shows nothing wrong with my brain via imaging. They take me into a hospital wing and leave me restrained to the gurney. All the beds in the staging area are taken so I am made to wait sort of left to the side of a hallway.

I look at the clock on the wall. It fascinates me. I begin thinking about the scene in *Fight Club* where Edward Norton is reading magazines in the basement about body parts in the third person.

I'd had stomach issues for months. They were from drinking. However, I begin to internalize, "Jack's raging gall bladder." I begin to try to connect that movie scene to myself, my stomach pains and enlightenment. It is all just utter madness.

2 men I'm not sure are watching me or not begin talking to me. I begin laying into my theory of black oppression and I believe I am enlightened. The words flow through my mouth and connect amazingly. It seems I've solved an issue that's plagued thinkers for generations while psychotic in a hospital wing strapped to a gurney.

The restraints are tight around my wrists. It's been an hour and I ask the men with whom

I was speaking if I can have them loosened a little and maybe have a glass of water. They act immediately to help me.

I'm swaying in unknown territory. The waves are coming and going. My life is up in the air. What will happen to me? What is going on? Why am I being treated in this particular clinical fashion?

You have to remember I don't know anything about mental illness in that moment. I assumed St. Vincent's was a destination for a pep talk before release. I assumed my pain and mental state was just a common experience for someone having a hard time with life. Now, I'm not so sure that is a good explanation given how everyone's reacting to me. I think I'm scared, but the lack of certainty of what's happening to me is palpable.

The question revolving my mind becomes just that. An intense uncertainty around the question, what is happening to me?

I lie on the gurney by myself for hours and hours. Once in awhile someone will come and inform me they're looking for a bed in a hospital. I wait patiently. It's all I can do.

No one comes to tell me I'm OK. No one explains anything about what is happening to me. It is the worst I've felt in my entire life and any information or comfort is just not happening.

I get word by night-time that there's a bed open at Columbia Presbyterian in White Plains. I'm wheeled back into the ambulance and taken away.

Waiting for intake I'm seated in a giant hallway with thick wood structural beams. The doors are made for giants to pass through. Columbia strikes me as old and knowing. I look up at a beautiful stained-glass window and hover in my desperation for a moment. My giant is near. It follows wherever I go.

On the psych ward I cry my 3rd day. My head hurts, I'm confused, I'm delusional, I'm catatonic for periods of time. It is very painful non-stop in everything. The first week I stare at paintings and write in my notebook.

Fragments of the Ward

Monday

I'm in front of a panel of doctors, alone. The chair in the center of the room is tiny. It looks like the loneliest chair in the world. Don't want to sit there. Don't fit. They start asking questions. "What brought you here?"

Waviness starts. I know I'm about to cry, I feel it forming around my eye muscles. I'm embarrassed. I answer.

"I wasn't good enough. I tried so hard. I tried. So hard. But I wasn't good enough." Tears begin, I look away. "I couldn't do it. I just, wasn't enough." 2 doctors are crying.

I know I'm in a psychiatric hospital. I make doctors cry. I feel horrible. Not much else I am certain of.

Samantha is my therapist. She joked about missing graduation by one credit. She's kind.

Tuesday
Awful vivid dreams from Seroquel.

Wednesday
Day 3. I scream and cry. It goes on for 20 minutes. It is a complete purge. Everyone on the floor knows I'm in the box from hearing me earlier. I sit with my back against the wall stifled in misery.

Thursday
Stared out the window and meditated and prayed to get through this. My head hurts for some reason. The continuance of performing good acts. My face hurts, temples are squeezed, my head is in pain, the pain is tolerable. Whatever's happening it's good, even in its intolerableness. Battling depression.

That was a violation of space. That much coddling repulses me. My parents. This is a very different feeling. This is pushing away. It's tougher.

Friday
   Emotional. Lost the ability of speech, again. Mom cries. Dad concerned.

Saturday
   Awoke calm. Wrote a poem:

February

The future looking
outside of the ward
at the bricks and
snow covered yard
visible for only the day
remains beside me
looming and pensive
when the nurse enters
bringing an order
of the day.

   Told by the doctor to look in the mirror and say what he calls, affirmation: "I am a person with a mental illness."

Saturday

A young lady from the church with a nervous disposition came today. I've never heard the word "coping skill" before, but she teaches them. She stays for 45 minutes. Coping skills are our main defense against extreme discomfort.

I can't help but notice an odd choice of painting on the wall. It's Edward Hopper's, "Office at Night." Hopper paintings expand on pressure, loneliness and isolation of city life. Why is this painting on the psych unit?

Sunday

Mood: relaxed, pretty good

Cognition: thoughts of helping myself, thoughts of being paranoid.

Wednesday

Danny and Conor are going to visit later after class, 6:30ish, and they'll be bringing food.

I terrified them. Dan cried and Conor scowled. Both fearful.

A wise man I spoke to yesterday disappeared. He told me he doesn't have long to live.

Monday

I use the pay-phone. I call Eric Mendenhall. He answers. I'm confused. We talk about music.

Sam's getting me moved to the cognitive therapy area of the hospital. There's no telling what might happen from this point.

I'm excited. She tells me everyday won't feel this amazing, so I should expect turbulence, some ups and downs, no more than the average human being expects. What is expected from the average human being?

Wednesday

Emotions flying everywhere, definitely not. Why do pieces of my past keep going through my mind?

Lost in emotions. People value their sanity more than they value an intense emotional experience they can get lost in, most of the time.

I hum Louis Armstrong and Duke Ellington's version of "Mood Indigo." Perhaps when I can go no lower there's music. Picasso.

He is dead. I do not know why except some awful markings he showed me around his ribcage.

Friday

My head hurts probably from all the delusional thoughts I've been having. Self-knowledge. What does helpless feel like?

Scott understands something hardly any of the other workers do, the empathy response. Without this the ward patients are surrounded and controlled by indifferent strangers.

I write psychotic philosophy most of the day. I'm trying to escape catatonia. (This is a catatonic person trying to overcome catatonia. May only be of interest to research.)

I write this note:

"A person yields to time's passage or finds the fluidity of time an inexorable problem one is stymied in. To push back at the situation one is contained within, to attempt to join oneself into the current exchange, or just bluntly to open oneself back up to the ongoing discussion, both hearing and responding, feeling and empathizing will counter-pressure the person completely within time.

"Moving to combat that sense of disorientation with the world leaves people all the more fixated with the things immediately before them, and these become more obstacles then relations with the momentary eclipse of human exchange.

"Standing your ground however invites the same disorienting effect and drives the person into a state of near panic, wholly insecure within the passage of time he sees only the shifting or rupture between people and notices the dire state is both created by him and by the external volume and violence of exchange. He has no emotional response for this only the crawling back into a prior catatonia. Not by an act of will nor by silently observing can one re-orient themselves within the social flux."

Jane arrives with cookies Cat baked. I'm grateful. When my visitors leave I am always terrified I'll never have the same relationship with them again after what they've seen here.

Friday

Daniel, Scott, Greg and some of the others who are level 3 patients are outside shooting hoops. 2:00, I believe is the time allotted for outdoor activities. While I am excited about my parents coming I cannot get overly excited about this one fact. Looking for equilibrium.

Saturday

I have Bi-Polar Disorder NOS. Invega feels like I have dirt in my head.

Roommate Dan had Electroconvulsive Therapy. Came back in wheelchair, soaked, head hanging. Despondent.

Psych Unit starting to feel normal. Invega calms me. Sam is by my side a lot. I appreciate her. Made her cry. She is so helpful.

Today. Tiger talks. The media is buzzing, every station is debating the man. What a sad state when the entire world is watching a golfer's off the field issues. Golf, that sport.

Anguish. My head hurts. Sam said every day wouldn't feel as good as yesterday did, but writing helps. Writing helps communicate how I feel, and the closer your message is to how you actually feel, the closer you are to the truth.

I socialize to find something to write.

Tuesday

I'm told Sam has been moved to another floor. I am hurt. I feel vulnerable. I'm feeling much better, still. I write a poem:

There's a woman who comes to see me
With a gold head, and a mind that ticks
Like a damn clock
She's my therapist that ya'see
But she listens and a woman can
Seem so endearing to a man
In my situation

But there's a woman that comes to see me
Ya'see
And she woke me up with a bang!
And now that I'm talking
She's into something that I can't
Do anything with

There's a woman on the other end
And it comes to that, gold headed girl

There's a woman who comes to see me
~~And she's~~
Today
And she's not going to be here
Today.

Football! It is early December. I am ecstatic to get some fresh air. I jump and make running throws. The others are impressed by my athleticism! I relish this chance to stretch my legs and smell clean air.

More friends visit. David brings pasta with chicken. Beats stinking beans and hospital meat.

Happy.

When my parents arrive I will treat them to a tour of the facility. Anthony has been very cordial and attentive to all my needs, but he may not be on duty. Charles and Daniel are here, Derrick and the nursing staff all deserve thanks. My roommate is somber a lot of the time but he could use a pat on the back.

Doctors tell me I'm progressing good. We talk about discharge potentially soon.

I talk to the social worker with Mom and Dad. We're planning follow-up treatment back home in Upstate, NY.

Wednesday
Day 17. Released.

Hometown

When I got home to my parents in Upstate, NY I felt almost immediately the return of acute psychosis. There wasn't the support of doctors anymore. Couple that with the loss of routine and no stability anymore. A loss of how to live like a person. You could say of course, we all wake up and go about our business, but for me the mental pain and psychosis leave me no room to adjust back to life in Upstate. It's almost as if I'm re-learning how to function as a human being beset with this Psychotic Disorder.

My discharge plan is to attend the Adult Partial Hospitalization Program, in Rochester, NY, and to also locate a psychiatrist in the area to provide medication administrative oversight and psychotherapy treatment. While I wait for this to start there's just no cohesion to my days anymore. I sleep, eat and lay my body *face-in* to the couches backrest for hours.

My dad drives me the first day to the out-patient program. I cannot drive some days from the disorientation of psychosis. I arrive in a state of disorientation that feels like an anvil in my skull. The couches are plasticky–easier to clean–and my iPod plays music as I contemplate the terror of talking to people around me and the fact I feel the way I do while in public.

The first group is a check-in session where you go around the tiny room of 9 to talk about how you feel. I cannot explain how the intensity was ratcheted up waiting for my turn, but it felt like standing directly behind the engine of a 747 as anxiety blew my head back making a 2-foot impression in the wall. By the time it's my turn I'm talking about cutting zits off my face with scissors–so just picture me 2 weeks estranged from a psychotic break striving to become aware of core beliefs to explain my predicament. The truth is I'm unrecognizable to anyone, and strangers are visibly unsettled by my daily check-in.

So this is a new beginning, not the kind you hope for, but, all the same, I acknowledge the fact I will have no quality of life for many years. When you have a psychotic break you have to learn how to live again. I don't know who I am. A common experience after a break is to have a damaged self, I also experience myself as a lost identity.

Terror comes with Anxiety Disorder and Bi-Polar Disorder with Psychotic Features taking swings individually or more often together. What I'm left with is life that just continues, and a new something that I don't understand.

Time, our most precious resource. Time is not valuable anymore. Slogans like, live each day like it's your last, or Carpe Diem seem to be sick jokes for people who have the ability to experience a pleasant emotion. Years of this like bags chucked into the garbage truck and compressed, taken to the dump just gone–all that un-lived raw time takes its toll.

I get emotional watching an 80's Brat Pack film called *St. Elmo's Fire*. It stars: Emilio Estevez, Judd Nelson, Ally Sheedy, Andrew McCarthy, and Demi Moore as a stick-together pack of young adults who frequently celebrate at St. Elmo's Bar–who navigate the world post-college together. When I watch it's like I should be pictured somewhere. There should be a photo of me in SoHo at somebody's apartment in a suit riffing on the work-world and its vagaries, or shedding some tears of relationship loss, a day trip to Rockaway beach for sun and swimming, or the existential housecleaning of carving your own place out in the world. It's just not my experience, I know this.

What I see is what happened in a way that my college friends might have lived. Leaning on each other as they grow with each other as peers and developing a sense of self together. The idea of being a young adult at the St. Elmo's Bar draws me in as some string of experiences I'll never have. What it was actually like to live your twenties must have been a blast, or maybe that's how everyone sees it who was not privy to actually being there. I spent the better half of my twenties in despondent over-medicated isolation.

The medication pummels me and bystanders would probably side-step my face for fear I'm a meth-head. Some days I never really wake-up.

"Time to get up!" my mom yells up the stairs.

I hear her as a faint background noise. This sedation is so heavy I don't know if I can.

Half an hour later it is 3 PM.

"David, it's TIME to get up!" Mom yells louder.

I can't do another day of this. I don't want to have to do another day of this. I'm being yelled at and I'm 22 years old. I'm not a kid. I'm not sure who knows just how hard it is to want to live. There's nothing for me, awake. There's nothing for me in this world to care about.

I reach down for the pail of ice water I've left a rag in. The antipsychotic medication I take at night leaves me incoherent and sedated until 7:00 PM. Several times a month, around 7:00, I can convince myself I want to try to have a life. I must rack my brain for a solution to the sedation.

My hand dips into the pail of ice water I've positioned next to my bed and I press the freezing rag into my face. My bedding wets and the water slips down my neck to create a disagreeable sensation. I get up.

I'm trying but these drugs are killing me.

The best analogy for the sedation: it's as if gravity works against you acutely. Gravity surrounds your entire body and a hand is holding you back against a chair. You may wriggle but you'll never rise. The sun begins to lower in the sky when I am fit to start my day. I have not moved to perform daily ablutions. The thing is I'm not dumb from the drug. I fully understand the need for productivity but this physical immediacy to climb out of it and do stuff is difficult.

I imagine mud and slime has the same consistency as my inaction. On these drugs you might think that 30 minutes of movement is a tall task and if by the end you feel the same way (symptomatic and sedated), what would be the point of getting out of this chair. If you need to know, there isn't a reason. You can't.

There are certain abilities humans possess we can take for granted like the ability to read, write, and speak. Psychosis is an impaired contact with reality, and that was my experience when I pick up a book, only to see a big block of symbols on a page. My eyes shuffle down the ledger but I don't *read*. How have you imagined this before? That my mind doesn't process sentences. It feels like the fairy-tales of science fiction I loved as a teenager. My written skills suffer as bad as my reading.

Not only can I not read or write–I can't think. **Disorganized Thinking** is a cognitive symptom. It's **not** this, "Should I go to the park. I did a chore today. I went to the park yesterday. Do chores need to be done before going to the park?"

It is this, "Volume displacement is calculated by measuring an oval. I ate tacos with a cholo. No, I never did that. But I blew into that bong one time. So embarrassing."

It's so overwhelming when my thoughts circle and circle in this wild whirlwind shooting nonsense around my frantic skull.

God, I need relief.

"I just want to write. I know I can do this. Focus." I tell myself.

"Concentrate."

There I am at my desk at midnight. My skull has little buzz-saws fidgeting around inside it. I'm hyper-anxious with heavy depression.

The streets are damp as cars pass and churn the water. The lamp glow outside is fogged and as I lift my eyes which have been pressed so hard into my sleeves it forms bright crosses as my eyes readjust focus. Outside, out there, it's dark. I've seen the daylight for 3 hours today and this lack of sun leaves me buzzed with depression.

I've been holding a pen for 10 minutes staring at a sea-shell.

"Just a catch-phrase. That's all."

"Concentrate."

"Sea-shells."

"Sea-shells all seen shelter."

"No."

5 minutes pass.

"Sea-shells wave like chips."

"Fuck."

"Sea-shells… Sea-shells…"

"Sea-shells… "

"Fuck. I can't."

My reality is one of a quiet war I keep to myself. I fight it with every ounce of my strength to get somewhere. When you check the facts today I took no actions, but that didn't stop me today from feeling like a 12-hour shift at Dairy Queen where you got punked by your manager for being 10 minutes late and the dishwasher quit. Somewhere you have no idea where it even begins, I say.

You can't compare this to a hangover, a bad day, a break-up, or some pain rooted in a cause. The pain is not causal. You wear the pain like you wear your crawling skin and skeleton. You wear it like your face and yellowing teeth. You wear it like we all wear a brain stuffed inside a shell of bone. It doesn't come off, sober-up, mend things with the boss, move on. If you asked me to just get over it I would say, "Tell me how, please. I want to not feel this way." The truth is, short of a lobotomy there's absolutely nothing I can do after a psychotic break to have a good day anymore. The prognosis of a psychotic break isn't something you work on to feel better soon. You're privy to pure un-lived raw time where you are damn near powerless.

No doctor ever bothered to broach the subject of how today was going to be a good day. All I hear are the same refrains:

acceptance, distress tolerance, week-end planning and safety check-ins.

How can I know where I'm going? What is the positive outcome I keep hearing about? What does a person who can't always think, or read, write and sometimes speak do to make improvements, and what are improvements? With what and how?

The only thing I think to try is to think my way out of it.

Therapy Session .02
First Year After Psychotic Break

"David you need to get out of your head."

"I know, but…how do I do that?"

"What's happening with the job search? Have you been pursuing work?"

"I have. Or I mean, I interviewed. It's at Wilson Farms as a cashier."

"That's great!" she says sharply.

That will get your mind off your thoughts. You need something to do. To get out of your head."

I don't know what she's talking about. I'm panicked there's something wrong with me.

Janet's my psychiatrist and she's blunt in our sessions. I'm in her office which is a separate extension of her home, as usual talking through my kaleidoscope of thoughts that cause me to occasionally stop myself. Feel confused. Janet can see my face and sense my anxiety enveloping the room.

"I know it's hard to handle. You have a very severe mental illness, David. You're doing the right thing being here in treatment. It's a start."

"What if I tried meditation or something…?"

"The last thing you want is meditation. Your anxiety will get worse."

I don't understand her. Why not just try meditation?

"Let's talk about the medication. How are you doing on the Zyprexa? Have you noticed any improvement in mood or otherwise?"

"I feel tired all day. I lie on the couch. The effect is strong. The drug makes it hard staying awake."

"The job will give you energy and something to focus on. There's going to be an adjustment period to starting the drug you're on. You have to get used to it.

"In the old days this type of drugs used to be a lot harder to tolerate. You're on what's called a 2nd generation Anti-psychotic. It's not well understood how the drugs work, but they work. You need medication right now. We just need to find the right one or a cocktail."

"I know I need to continue trying these medications, but isn't there a natural way of doing this?"

"You're going to try and get off them, every person does and the consequences of doing that are usually very severe. That may sound harsh but it's inevitable."

I freeze. I've thought about it before, many times.

The room is occupied by a hundred exotic lamps that dangle and occupy every surface or nook. The lamps are illuminated or dulled depending on if the sun shines through the yard into our windows. A mellow St. Bernard lies on his molded pad of knotted brown cotton, and then at odd times will approach to breathe on my hands and drip slobber which also tends to stop me. I have an ever-present awareness of him and for that bulging black-fungus gum that hangs, and that inseverable string of saliva that swings from its jowl features sometimes swinging itself back over into its own teeth multiple times in a 30-minute session.

"My head hurts all the time. I feel these waves and this confusion."

"How would you describe them?"

"Like right now, it's floating and I feel uptight, was it something in my past, or something wrong with me that causes this…"

"You have a medical condition, David. A serious one. It's how your brain works and it's part genetics and part environmental. I talked to your parents with your permission and we've been discovering some of your family members may have been undiagnosed mentally ill."

This is news. Of course, my grandfather walked out on 6 children.

"It doesn't mean you did anything bad to cause it, you're overthinking. Let's focus on right now. If you notice an improvement on the Zyprexa let's continue with it, are you OK with that?"

I really don't want these drugs.

"Yes, I noticed feeling a little better."

We spend the rest of 15 minutes talking and we end things cordially, then she says:

"David, don't show up to therapy drunk again."

"I…uhh, yes."

I'm fired from Wilson Farms. 2 weeks of fumbling around the register and fucking up everything. I look like a meth-head on Zyprexa.

No one at The Westchester Hispanic Coalition would recognize this person.

"I thought that might happen. It was too soon."

"I don't know who I am anymore. What happened to me?"

Janet scales back.

"Let's focus on what we can do today."

How are the… How are the… How are the… How are the… How are the…

I can't write. I still try.

desperateness holds me
and my whole body
feels it
what is there to say
i long for peace
hoping that in time it will
what prevails tomorrow couldn't know
god but you feel it
long as the sun

shriveled
like a fig
son of a bitch
go on

Live at home. Don't work. The booze and weed helps everything drown out. I'm not too proud to admit I'm helpless. Do my college friends think of me? No one calls. Doesn't matter, wouldn't be able to answer. I'm fucked up. I'm not someone they would ever hold in esteem or want to talk to.

"David we tried, but I'm not the best equipped to handle cases as severe as yours," Janet says.

I'm too severely mentally ill for Janet's care. I'm sent to a clinic for low-functioning patients in Henrietta, NY, called Strong Ties. I get a therapist and start treatment, again. From the beginning.

Nice to meet you David….What symptoms…What drugs have you…What would you like me to call you, David or Dave…Have you had any suicidal thoughts…Yes. I know this is our first session but I want to try…

OK.

What are your goals in therapy…?

I don't know.

Sunless

Why then bear us into a world
Sunless and freak
Lie makers meet and instruct
The freight of heaven
Made to feel, made out of the deal
Yet offer, cruel godless flickering
Death with certainty, yet strength to examine
What fruitless world then turns this action
Made to look at what has happened
But yet, ah, is a life of madness before death fair?
Will the mountain clear in the lofty air this despair?
Or rare, will love enchant a man's system,
To revolutionize a mind of loathsome derision?
Fair then or not, it's clear we cannot know time dearly
But fair despite for born we feel
Enough of the hours to slit under our chins
The option at last to exit the putrid world once
Is the life of madness before death not worth living?
Fair or not, we're made out of the deal
Even with death we do not reason
Utter then callously,
With madness living is excretion.

"Just let go."
"Just sink to the bottom."
"Don't go up."

"Do this."

"It's getting colder."

PART 2

The Storm Is a Normal State

Aftermath

2012.

Seasons go by.
3 years have passed since my admittance into Columbia Presbyterian.

Vague attempts at poems strewn everywhere mixed with coping skill worksheets. The notebooks from Columbia Presbyterian begin to accrue that faint dust perceivable only to someone who picks one up. My room is full of notebooks. 10 or 12 are filled with observations and hopes for freedom from mental illness. A lot of these notebooks are places where words and attitudes express a time when I couldn't escape the "locked-in" experience of psychosis. The books contain sentences broken off mid-stream. Many pages are tales of frustration, among the letters to friends abandoned out of fear. Then there are the statements from the panic room of the mind that would puzzle or alarm any reader.

Much is the same.

The idea that doing nothing gets you nowhere is false, because it took no action to accustom myself to life in a horrible mental place. The method is to exist through pure raw time. There is no substitute for the benefit of just survival time spent in early recovery. Through time spent mentally ill I am not better; it's just that I'm in some sick way used to always being symptomatic. That demented incomprehension of what happened to me, well, "What has happened to me!!?" doesn't occur anymore. This is not to say I accepted my mental illness or applied myself to recovery much just like this poem. My landscape is still bleak.

I used to smile
some people said a lot
then I grew up
in a shadowy forest
the lakes in winter were bleak
the fall was lonely
and I could not change it,
not like the seasons adjust
my new way of living
was permanently fixed
like the clock
five minutes to midnight

3 years of living with mental illness to become more coherent in writing, to read again, and with an increase in antipsychotic medication to find some stability. What antipsychotics actually do, I still have no idea. Their therapeutic use was discovered by accident.

I had to pass a psychiatric evaluation before admittance back to SUNY-Purchase. This took place in the summer of 2011.

I drove myself to the interview. Coasting down Route 17, I felt aspirations of picking up where I left off. A Purchase return would mean

I could complete those last 17 credits and graduate. I had taken medical leave from this campus of brick box-shaped buildings, the architectural style of brick brutalism. The outdoor walkways to class were given roofs to funnel the breeze on summer days and cool you, but I can only remember the year of my psychotic break as the freezing wind tunnels this design unknowingly creates.

The first time I visited Purchase I was with my dad. We pulled up by the theatre building and saw a young man sprawled out in the grass. That sunny day, Pops remarked, "This might be a good fit for you." Indeed, it feels similar to that day as I pull into the parking lot. The grass is green and it is the start of summer. I make my way to the counseling center.

My therapist and psychiatrist supplied their own psychiatric evaluations in favor of my return, but I will see a school psychiatrist to make the final decision.

I'm confused
What does he mean?
Why is he repeating the same question 3 times?

I answered him.

Why is the answer unsatisfactory?

What does it matter where I live?

He already asked that

He already asked that

Is there something wrong with me?

Just continue!

I'm panicking

I'm anxious.

Talk normal, damn it.

What the hell….

Of course I'm ready, don't you read the reports?

Just go with it.

What is happening?

I'm better now. Why can't you see that?

Quit talking in that tone!

I'm having a fucking panic attack.

Accept the emotion.

You're not talking to an invalid!

It's…

Over?

2 weeks pass before the letter arrives in the post. I sit down to read it. I feel my heart whacking at my chest as the letter unfolds.

"OK, OK."

Then it reads, "We regret…"

Impact.

I read the letter despite the mood-altering bomb that leaves a depressive buzz.

I set the letter down and put my palms to my forehead. I start thinking,

"I thought I was better. What's wrong with me? What don't I know? What don't I understand?"

I fall back on the couch. My eyes close. My mother comes to get the news, but sees the news in my face and moves to console me.

Denied.

Denied.

But the bigger issue I feel now is,

"Does this get better?"

Life Goes On

There's more talk in therapy of the future like getting a job or joining a volunteer organization.

I join The National Alliance on Mental Illness Rochester Chapter, but my volunteerism is short-lived after attending an awareness event where my anxiety left the other co-volunteer disconcerted. I chose to stop as my anxiety clearly was not manageable while representing an organization in public.

Ruby Tuesday hired me as a dishwasher. The suds and wrinkled hands and stings of hot plates went on for a year. I didn't make any friends because I did not speak to anyone apart from the muttered yes or no's. There were no social skills to speak of.

When I was around my friend Dan, I could converse with him, but I always felt frustrated by my ineptitude at socializing which he was understanding about more so than others. From ages 21-23, I could talk to high school friends and do the odd activity, but the impact of mental illness I felt every day and the drinking didn't stop.

Still no contact from college friends. Jane visited me though!

"You're my rock, Jane!"

"That's nice, but remember we have to be our own rock," Jane said.

I feel confusion. I put my phone down.

Jane's in my corner. It feels good to have someone there for me. My emails are raw and painful, but she takes time to respond even while I'm sure they are difficult to read. Jane draws a boundary at one point.

"I'm here to listen and to support you, but I need you to understand that I'm not your therapist."

I feel hurt.

The hopelessness I feel and victimhood of chaotic mental health is one of the ugliest mental states you can imagine. As you feel totally incapable. That people object to the total of you.

I was afraid
of you
my friend

And in that way
Afraid
Of what I am

I am no bad person
I am what I am
Human

What of human,
But difference
Which becomes objection

So in people's reactions
I fear
what I am

And that is inferior, weak,
And I
I am full of shame

can I be
anything else
that would protect me

Help
Immunize
Me

Because I feel it sharply
Friend
And I am afraid

That all my failings
Lead to one objection
The total that is me

The quest for help really becomes *someone please be available, that's all I ask*. Though I wouldn't have the strength to ask that. Just to know I have someone, if I could even bring myself to write or communicate with them, which often, I can't.

It would mean everything.

Unity Hospital

My first 3 years post-Columbia Presbyterian I've made a 2nd and 3rd trip to the Out-patient Treatment Program. I'm still in the dual-diagnosis program. Chadd and Amanda are especially kind to me and notice when I'm sober, keen to urge me on at how well I'm doing.

I relapse at a concert. Drive drunk. I wake up suicidal. I know it's going to kill me.

"I'll be honest with you, if you don't get sober, and don't do it right now, you'll be dead in a month. So imagine your family at your funeral, crying, looking down at your coffin."

Text From Robert

"So you went to a concert and decided to drink because you were at a concert? Did you drink because you wanted to or because you were at a concert?"

"Well I…I was at a concert so it was easy so I drank."

"Your new nickname is Concert Dave." (People laugh.)
People who are right

I am found naked in an empty bath-tub midway through a cigarette, a bottle of gin in my crotch. I am folding up in my sad helpless self of shame and 50 unprocessed experiences needful of feeling and understanding–sitting there in that loud-in-the-head and destructive I give no fucks feeling.

Dad finds me, he says, in a very sad way:

"Alright, son, let's get you out of here."

I relapse with alcohol and go off medication 3.5 years after Columbia Presbyterian. I stumble around the front yard with my hands squeezing my skull. Dad finds me.

"I need to go in. I need to go in now," I say. My father knows what to do.

I watch the scenery go by as we drive to Strong Memorial Hospital in Rochester. The day is so bright. Summer. We pass hillsides and the truck paths into fields where nature is growing back to cover the treads. Someone must think it's an ideal day for a hike. Somewhere a person is lying in the grass to admire the sky. Such a perfect day.

I drew a lovesong
Under the apple tree
Through the cutlass
Of the kaleidoscope
As my heart bespoke
Both common weeds and common folk
I fell asleep in my canoe
And drifted as the pollen flew...

I drew a lovesong
Under a mangled tree
At 3 o'clock in the afternoon heat
As the cicadas let out their purr of screech

I remember
running through the golden fields
As mother calls out "dinnertime!"
Dusk chasing at our heels

Under a mighty tree that stood alone
Falling in love with the pen
Often now, by age…

Often now…

I'm hearing the deep notes

It's classical.

Through the malaise of pain embroidered in
the light of the environment I turn to Papa.

"Papa."
"Yes," he said.
"How are you doing?" he asks.
"I don't know."

Papa keeps his poker face on so as not to
worry me. It's something to make your son feel
OK when it's not OK, because the illusion still
holds value.

Somewhere a person is just lighting up a charcoal grill.

My face rests on the door panel. I slot my cheekbone into just above the interior door handle, and I stay there until I feel a dull sting. I feel the tiny bumps and sicken from the slow pace of the car which is going 60 mph. I get closer to the hospital with each mile. The reality of the hospital starts to vibrate.

Going back again.

Fuck it.

It was just where Janet had prophesied I would end up. I'm in Unity Hospital looking for grace wherever the light touches the pane.

The floors of linoleum are yellow and white and refract the light to create a hazy feeling in the dim corridors at Unity. A worker guides me to a room with a 70's gurney that matches the 70's tile and tells me, "The doctor will be by in a little while." There's a blanket that is wafer-thin and 0% cotton that doesn't cover my 6'2" body unless I get in a fetal position and pin the blanket under my toes.

I feel distraught with only one action to cope with it and that is to lie motionless. I wait 3 hours alone until a worker brings a tray of food and mimes the same remark. Hours go by, alone. I begin to feel I am forgotten about. After 8 hours of waiting alone a doctor enters for a 7-minute consultation and I'm led to the psych unit.

I lie in my rectangular frame bed on a stiff mattress gazing at a tempered-glass window. I feel a sickly beauty in the air. It is calm as I stare at the window and think of what it's going to take. What do I have to do now that I'm back here at the hospital? I study the window with a whitish aura. I know what I must do.

I resign myself to the need for in-patient stabilization. I accept this need unconditionally.

Back again my friend.
Back to fucked.

Draft Excerpt:

My therapist is informed of my whereabouts.

Where am I?

Here, again.

Terror. I walk the hallways, it feels like slowed down frames, the shutter flick on a camera.

What happened? Here, again.

For 2 days I'm quiet. I keep to myself.

I've been hired and fired a few times. I've got meds. I still drink, that's why I might be here.

I'm here, again. Better make the best of it.

There's a group in the lounge area talking. I pull up a chair and listen.

I spend some time in the TV room watching *Law & Order* reruns then head back to sleep. Groups were good today. I'll keep reviewing these sessions, see what I can learn.

Next day I see the unit's head-psychiatrist Dr. Moose. He carries himself business-like with such brevity that it seemed like he might have known exactly what I was experiencing, and then again, might have had no idea at all.

He gives me a report of what he's seeing. Dr. Moose confirms I've had a psychotic episode. He draws up a good prognosis based on my behavior on the unit and with my compliance with medication and participation in group, he expects a shortened stay. We finish our brief chat and I spend some time in the lounge area staring at the wall.

I look out the window at Rochester.

People carrying on, cars stream by steadily as I watch through the mesh steel wondering when I'll get a cigarette and what out there will feel like again. If I'm ready.

Not much going on.

"You have a bad spirit on you." I took that to mean Regina's religious inclinations caused her to say such a thing. Regina is a young girl that claims she has conversations with god. Maybe she is hallucinating a thing on me.

I enjoy our conversation which veers from the supernatural to her non-compliance with medication, and her sultry unreflexive attitude that I observe during my stay is a positive distraction from the monotony. Though I feel disheartened that her actions will complicate any release back into circulation with the free-people's mental hospital of humanity.

Joe, I can tell is severely suicidal. It's his hyper-squeamish voice and hyper-sensitivity which betrays nothing but high tension and high stakes. He's a pastor albeit recent to the profession, and so he gives a mass in the rec room and I go to support him.

I continue to attend all the groups and participate. It's better to do your part here. I can learn from other patients as well.

I sit by myself in the lounge area on my 6th day.

All the things I've tried have failed. It's just like AA. You have to give up. Cease doing things your way. Your way is an abject failure. It's insanity. Now what should I do…

…..

…..

I give up. I'm going to do what they've been telling me to do. I'm doing it to a T. No shortcuts. I'll do all the work. I'm going to get sober. I'm going to try as many medications as I have to. Find a cocktail and get stable, and study recovery in-depth and gather as many coping skills as I can. I'm going to be my own advocate. I'm going to do what they've been telling me to do all along.

…..
…..

This is my decision. This or I will die.

Maybe it was my weariness. Maybe it was just my growing dislike for suffering. But for as long as I can remember I followed through with that decision.

I stay on at Unity for 10 days. I get a lot of healing done with other patients. A kind woman and fine listener remarks, "You're hurt," and I say, "Yes," and I feel the hurt and heal as we all take turns speaking about what brought us there. These were deep painful stories like a man confined to a wheelchair losing custody of his children, a man who hallucinated the Virgin Mary and fell apart from psychosis, a man with 2 black eyes and a bruised face from professional MMA with family trauma, a woman whose husband was in the military and was wrecked from stress. That impromptu joint patient-circle was a union of people with unique stories that felt the emotional safety of all of us and very much needed space to be heard.

A lot of healing gets done with other patients. If you sit a table across people talking, feel the conversation out. You might be one chair away from starting to heal a part of you.

Stare at a wall. You'll never see these people again.

Attend groups.

Most importantly, stock up on graham crackers and oranges when no one's looking. Make a stash in your room.

I'm released.

The prognosis is good.

My sister is there to pick me up.

I walk down the steps into more light than the unit supplied, and feel a sense of opportunity in front of me.

Even as the fresh air flows through my lungs I know there's much to do.

Post Unity

"I WILL BE YOUR SERVANT. WHATEVER YOU ASK OF ME, I WILL SERVE YOU FAITHFULLY! I WILL DO WHAT YOU ASK!"

In some deep and remote forest I scream at god.

The first days I spent outside Unity Hospital were full of such acute emotional distress I nearly became a Christian! I'm surprised I didn't kill myself, actually.

I stay sober 3 months and relapse. Following that relapse I got sober again and have been for 11 years and counting.

A great and lasting gift, what AA in my gruff blue collar community taught me was very simple: exactly how serious my situation with alcohol is.

I know in my bones I can't just have one.

Now that I'm hell-bent on recovery without shortcuts I follow the helpers' way, not mine.

You could say I was a man possessed after my stay at Unity. I just bought in to everything.

The Four Parts of Recovery

There were stacks of DBT, CBT and "Mental Health" worksheets from all my partial hospitalizations and getting deep into review began. I was familiar with coping skills such as: distraction, soothing, distress tolerance, acceptance and relaxation. This is my survival education from now on.

My mission is to create a recovery toolbox. What goes in it, tools. When I'm broken or symptomatic I'm now going to tune-up my mental health. Deep breathing is a tool. I learn correct breathing. Now it's part of my toolbox. Of course the point isn't knowing what a tool is; when you need it take it out and fucking use it.

Every day I use coping skills for whichever symptoms I am experiencing. Could be: anxiety, depression, mania, hearing voices (when under tremendous stress) or OCD.

Actively using a survival education is the start of symptom management. This is called being responsible for your mental illness. This is called accepting your mental illness on the grounds it's real and not going anywhere. I must live my life in that acknowledgement of reality with self-care because I have a mental illness. It's real.

1. Acceptance

I said the affirmation, "I am a person with a mental illness," just like they told me at Columbia Hospital. Living my life in acknowledgment of this reality was how I found acceptance. By that I mean, when I took on responsibility for managing my mental illness it was the acknowledgment that I had one.

When I lived that recovery lifestyle it allowed me to be intimate with the symptoms of my mental illness. Whereas before it was simple chaos, I made strides to embrace the illness and learn its ways.

I became so connected with Bi-Polar symptoms once with my friend Matt in the mall, I remarked:

"I got to get home soon Matt. You know how I'm so talkative and fun, yeah, that's because I'm a little manic. My mania is a 3.2 out of 10. So in about an hour or so it's going to flip into a 3.2 of depression and I have to prepare."

He had little concept of what mania meant, but I was right about the flip and severity.

Getting intimate with your illness is self-knowledge of illness. It's accomplished by taking responsibility for managing your mental health, every day. If you're in touch at the nitty-gritty level this facilitates some control over preparation of how to cope.

2. Recovery Stories

Another thing I did was comb websites for recovery stories so I could begin to believe it was possible for me too. These stories inspired me. I got academic and experimented with theoretical frameworks of recovery by contemporary psychiatrists. The stacks of them all neatly assembled and stapled together still sit somewhere in the room infused with light from which I now write.

The most dramatic shift was a sudden jolt of sustained stability that came with a full month of no alcohol. There were Bi-Polar symptoms but it felt as though my floor had risen in terms of keeping stable.

When I write "floor," I simply infer from it my capacity of relative safety; my mood will not descend past my floor, nor will my mania ascend my ceiling (mood). Medication, sobriety, are 2 whimsical movements of generating a finite space in which moods play. Some feel or mourn the loss of highest of highs, or learning from the lowest of lows. Usually a severely mentally ill patient will accept a space of play like this. The one I describe relative to my sobriety.

After Unity, not only was I hell-bent on recovery, I was resolved to try every medication. And, as you'd expect now, I did this.

3. Medication

I went to Rae, my psychiatrist, with unshakable determination to try every psychiatric medication she desired to use and fuck the side effects.

"Rae, what do you want to start me with? I'm open to anything."

Talk about a psychiatrist's wet dream

We began by pairing antidepressants with antipsychotics. We also experimented with dosages of a mood stabilizer I was on. It was heaven and hell. I never gave up even when I had miraculous improvements that were short-lived, or when going temporarily blind for Thanksgiving weekend.

My attitude became this: if you treat it comically it can't hurt you. I laughed when my vision was a colorful blur and I went to spear a turkey chunk but returning it to my plate it fell in my lap.

"David." Mom, I'm guessing, has a concerned look on her face.

"As Ray Charles said, 'Let the good times roll.'" I find the turkey chunk and just smile.

I taper off the mood stabilizer, but by Day 5 I'm really running with the joke. Locating things is hard, but I chuckle after taking 7 minutes to find the bathroom inside a McDonald's–a not altogether difficult feat most days. In fact most things provide a source of laughter anyway. I didn't know if my vision would come back. I assumed it would, but somehow if it didn't that would be funny too.

Kurt Vonnegut has recounted this story many times of the bombing of Dresden, hunkered down in a shelter with his fellow soldiers. As the bombing thundered above, one soldier asked, "I wonder what the poor are doing tonight?" No one laughed, but they were all glad he said it.

Humor sometimes hits the same when there's peril, at least to me anyway.

There were challenges with each antidepressant I took. Each followed the same pattern, 5 days of no effect, then the most significant mood improvement in my life. Then with it came insomnia. On the antidepressants I would let insomnia go for 7 days as I soldiered through in hopes the insomnia would abate.

It never did.

Didn't matter.

Go off it. A week of recovery time. Give me the next one. Prozac. 4-5 days of no effect, then a repeat of mood improvement. Then insomnia for 7 days. OK. Give me the next one.

Again.

Same result.

Again.

Same result.

Again.

Same result.

Finally there's one antidepressant taken at a baby dose which helps to keep me more stable without insomnia. Victory. What it took to be a punching bag and make progress I only thought of as not bitching out on recovery.

4. Self-Advocacy

The next phase was self-advocacy. When you engage in self-advocacy you are empowering yourself to manage your own treatment. Empowering yourself to manage your own treatment empowers you to progress in your recovery. When I feel empowered I make good decisions for myself. Sure I used to get my re-fills a day before they ran out, until I started not to and began looking at my insurance plan. Then I feel empowered to start learning the terms insurance companies use. When I get knowledge of the insurance language it empowers me to call insurance companies about questions I have. Empowerment begets more empowerment.

I calculated what every co-pay is on the 6 medications I take, and I keep a binder with reference to every medication and details of my insurance. I know what my insurance plan covers and I have confidence.

The starting point was I knew nothing. I have some insurance plan and it's through my parents. I show up at the pharmacy and hope they'll give me meds or I have to ask for 3 pills till my script I ordered late comes through. My parents keep hospital records and important documentation. Now so do I.

It's funny, now I'm watching yearly changes happening with Medicare that may affect me. That's real recovery in action.

I make informed decisions with my psychiatrist about what medications to try or stop based on actual evidence I supply. Now I call my psychiatrist when I'm overly-symptomatic and in danger. That's real recovery in action.

I became compliant to the mental health system unconditionally. What I was told I did. When I did this, symptoms and general quality of life got better. Then I kept on doing it.

This didn't all happen overnight. It was when I started to feel good that I liked feeling good. I did the next thing and the next thing and let professionals take recovery out of my hands, in a manner of speaking. Just follow, for now. That's it.

Work & Re-learning Socializing

I hadn't had sex or been close to anyone in years. You can starve for a spoonful, but the reality is without social skills or a mind you trust it's nearly impossible to be close with someone. At The Doubletree by Hilton I worked there 3 good years and was able to re-learn how to socialize.

My first week I stood in the lobby like a sentry only interacting when spoken to. People thought I was serious about work. The reality was I was pissing my pants and terrified to talk to them. See, I hadn't really made a friend in 7 years and my friends from the past had been out of my life. I put myself to the test in an environment where you're forced to develop some form of relationships when in the workplace.

"Hey man," Matt says.

"Hey."

"Hey man, welcome to The Doubletree," Matt laughs.

"Yeah."

"I was here when you turned your resume in. Do you remember?"

I suddenly do.

"It's good working here. You'll like it. Well, if I said **always** it would be a stretch." Matt laughs. "You'll like it."

"I'm excited to work here."

"Whoa, they got one. We got a company man. Haha. I'm just kidding"

With a serious face, "I went to school for Hospitality."

I begin to think Matt is going to be my closest friend here, already.

"That's cool."

"You don't say much. Well it's your first day. Relax man, you're going to do great. Haha."

I panic. When don't I?

There are 3 classic impairments of Schizoaffective Disorder: occupational, academic, and social. Here I am with an occupation. I'm able to read and write again. At the start of my Doubletree years I felt like I was not there to make friends. My sense was I hoped these people would just tolerate the fact I'm around them.

People will pass by me and say hello. I stand still. I'm glad they're friendly to the new guy. Matt is boisterous and always calls me over to talk about, whatever, whatever's on his mind. I admire how he speaks, so fluid, so carefree. It interests me how expressive people are and I think I long to express myself in that way, but I am disastrously awoken to my limitations each workday: broken sentences, long pauses, silence. I'm just not there yet. Is it hopeless?

Hold on, the more I interact with people I start to get more in the flow of talking. My responses are short or venture into long-winded deep statements. There really isn't much to my communication style, but people do tolerate me and even some call me over and smile during conversation which causes me to feel some elation of acceptance. Maybe there's a chance of doing something about these inhibitions/impairments.

At college on my birthday 10 people bought me a bottle of liquor apiece. There were too many friends to stuff into that tiny dorm who wanted to be with me. I have another memory of returning from New Orleans and showing up that night to be tackled by 10 people in a massive reunion hug of joy.

That person felt gone for good. However, maybe all's not lost. In David Whitwell's book, "*Recovery Beyond Psychiatry*," he points out we're never going to be the same after a major mental health upheaval. He says recovery as promised through medical model treatment will never make us the people we once were, and not to expect that, but that the achievement of improvement is possible through different "non-specific factors."

Non-specific factors include new relationships or a new job. The effects of these non-specific factors can't be quantified by Mental Health at large. That's to say, you don't put "make a great friend" or "get the job you love" on a recovery action WRAP sheet. It's just not something you plan for because it's what life throws you. Whitwell says these non-specific factors might have more to do with sustained recovery than any psychiatric intervention.

The fatal psychotic break had never made my social skills feel so final. The experience had turned a very social person into being a dishwasher at Ruby Tuesday who does not speak. 3 months in that cramped kitchen with people feet away, and aside from a whispered "yes" or "OK" at Ruby's, people have no idea who I am or what sort of developmental issue I had.

When I randomly unleashed a freestyle rap with another dishwasher a waitress leaned over in shock, "That's more words than I've heard you say since you started here." I just stay quiet feeling unease.

You can spend your early 20's sourcing yourself for the answer to social immobility and only finding dead-end explanations. Sometimes feeling caught in a loop.

But I want to fix myself.

To want to fix yourself is actually the beginning of recovery in some sense.

It was a simple job to shuttle guests and perform ordinary tasks around the hotel. Bring a toothbrush to a guest, stuff like that.

The first thing I thought of was to stand at my bellman's desk in down-time and write a positive message to myself. Then I approach our front desk agents and attempt a brief conversation. Inevitably a guest would arrive and break this up, at which time I bee-lined back to my bellman's desk to write a follow-up nurturing message. Oftentimes they looked like this.

Before approaching #1: "*I can do this. I'm a good person and someone they would probably like to get to know. I know I fail a lot. I can do this. Alright, go!*"

Back at desk #1: *"That wasn't awful. It's something to build on. I was a little 'crazy' but I got to keep going. I'm in a learning process. It takes time. I can do it."*

Before approaching #2: *"I am learning how to be OK with myself. I'm doing OK. If I keep applying myself I'll be OK again."*

Back at desk #2: *"I'm learning how to talk with people. I think Elle likes me. I will continue to push myself. I'm not worthless. I'm not an awful person. I'm in a process."*

I did this for a whole year.

As lame as it sounds, I thought of nurturing myself like an inner child. What I did was simply be nurturing to myself. It's not rocket science. You can be in a room full of people and not be ***there***. I had been very accustomed to isolating like that.

I began to get in the flow of talking. It would seem taken for granted that you wake up every day and have a conversation with people whom you encounter. It's kind of not thought about for most people to do that. Talking alone was hard for me. Having been isolated in my head I didn't have a heck of a lot of skill of how to talk. A lot of the time I went in a direction that missed a social cue and just began down a road that caused people confusion or to hesitate later when I was around, about interacting with me. But I had hope.

After months of nurturing and interaction with co-workers, besides guests who loved me when I donned the cap of customer service rep (I always seem to perform wonders when it's my job), I became a passable talker. Liz, my co-worker, had a visible anxiety disorder, so I began to mention things about my mental illness here and there to her. Robert, the very friendly and profane maintenance guy, was always telling me I'm gay and I felt close with him breaking balls over cigs.

I never became a wonder-kid socializer. People seem to have an agreeable relationship with me though. People liked me, but still I mean, c'mon, living isn't about toeing the line of being able to talk. It's found in the free-flowing, care-free expression I once had and so longed for.

Yet, still I went nurturing, socializing, trying and trying to recover my life. Slowly the grip of being caught in my mind loosened.

By year 2, I began flirting with Cassandra in the back office.

The route of standard shame is easy to articulate. People with mental illness may believe they do not have a medical condition. They may believe mental illness is a freak syndrome and they're some insane deviation of nature. In my case I'd decided Schizoaffective Disorder was unacceptable and not to be talked about. I never thought twice about it. People living with mental illness may let society subvert them into believing this. What I'm saying is, at some point there is this conversion wherein you believe having mental illness is disgraceful.

Vertex is a dim Goth club lite with positive accepting energy from its regulars and those of all walks of life that trickle in–probably secretly or outwardly cherishing the comfort of that wide open atmosphere. The owner who is also the bartender remembers the name of everyone who ever ordered a drink, and got their name in the process. It's been 4 years since I went to Vertex, only had 4 conversations ever with her but if I walked in tonight she'd smile and say, "Hey Dave, non-alcoholic beer?" Mind you she started stocking NA Beer just for me. This memoir if it fails to include such a digression into her wonderful person is an abject waste of time for me to sit here and write.

Liz invites me to Vertex often to dance to the pound and grind of Marilyn Manson tracks like, "The Beautiful People," or drum-impact of industrial techno tracks. These invitations sit well with me. Then it seemed I was close to my old self. Maybe the closest since my psychotic break.

Mental State at Work

I challenged my anxiety and OCD with comic strips of my own stick figures. The faux marble bellman's desk with swirling green and white design felt the tapping of a pen constantly. I'm there writing constantly with a purpose.

The bellman's desk is really in lunar orbit. "The stars like diamonds, atoms as massive as suns, universes smaller than atoms." In my polyester dress-shirt with magnetic name-tag I'm really searching the frontiers of my mind for a new life, one that is not dominated by symptoms and hyper self-awareness.

My happiest discovery was laughter as an effective diffuser. When I was OCD or catastrophizing I found that my comic strips of stick figures that illustrated the absurdity of my worry-towards-death, or worry-towards-insanity, could almost be completely expunged by laughter. The worries played off going insane. When I would draw my thoughts out in funny scenarios, I found that I was catastrophizing things extremely unlikely to occur.

That my worry was very unlikely or just preposterous didn't always register, but my comic strips inevitably turned sarcastic, ridiculous, or absurd because that's the nature of catastrophic thinking I suppose. I would lift my head from the comic strip with a smile and go back to work.

Intrusive thoughts were a symptom of my illness I struggled with. These came as suicidal, homicidal, or plain disgusting thoughts or impulses. I picked up this symptom at age 23, and I was extremely worried, panicked and preoccupied with the content of these thoughts and impulses. Man, that was an adventure into some shit I didn't know how to come to grips with.

Janet, my first therapist, gave me all sorts of confirmation that I'm not the type of person to murder, rape, etc. And I'm not, I know this for human purposes (which is all the certainty you can ever attribute to human behavior). She remarked great fathers need to go sometimes to a separate room when their daughters are in puberty. This shocked me and in a fucked-up way comforted me temporarily.

At the end of the memoir I'll take you through the process of contemplation and truth of the dark, but here at age 25 I don't have the clarity to even use my mind to get at deeper truth. Nowadays I have nothing to hide because I looked at everything I had hidden. I'm blessed to have the strength of mind to free myself of shame and now bravely looking into the truth of the dark, I don't have anything that needs truly to be hidden.

The intrusive thoughts were really debilitating in my mid-20's. Salvation came in a little book called *The Imp of the Mind*, which laid out how OCD sufferers often deal with a range of repetitious and terrifying thoughts and impulses. It rang true that those who feel distraught, guilty or ashamed of these thoughts and impulses were people that can take comfort in knowing that for "human purposes," they are not those who act on them. That's to say the indication here is, that those having the reactions of shame, guilt or terror are those people unlikely to act on them anymore than the next person.

I found that satisfactory. Air to breathe. When I had some space to breathe from the shame, fear and guilt I created a mantra for dealing with the emotional responses to the intrusive thoughts.

"I have a mental illness, that is a symptom, I am not my illness, and it doesn't follow that I would follow through with those thoughts."

What this mantra did was lessen the emotional reaction I was having to the thoughts and feelings. Think, if you have an intrusive thought and freak-out emotionally, is that emotional freak-out going to make the thoughts worse or better? The freak-out gives it staying power. My mantra didn't eliminate them completely. However the reason I was suffering so acutely had more to do with the emotional reaction to the intrusive thoughts.

If someone asks me about suicidality, homicidality or things of that nature I don't shirk. These are human thoughts and feelings. You can try and "live, laugh and love" all you want but you're still a human.

"Gotta go now."

"Gotta go, gotta go."

I pick up my pace heading to the bathroom.

I enter and check for people,

"All clear."

"Please, please let this not be voices."

I sit on the pot and close my eyes.

The room is silent. 10 seconds go by.

"Oh my god, I'm good. I'm good."

I leave the bathroom and slip right back into the workday.

A day comes when I'm crouched against a wall having a cigarette. I look over the wasteland of suburbia with Jimmy John's and Ho Ho wrappers in the bushes and it just feels right. I have a job, friends, and even accept some people don't like me, you can't help that. I think I'm a success to overcome meeting the demands of a full-time job. The fact is not every Schizoaffective patient is going to ever achieve occupational stability. I did.

I left The Doubletree on good terms with everyone there. People came up to me or cracked jokes with a telling smile. I was going to be missed? When I started here my goal was be tolerated. Just as a side-note, for the first time in my mentally ill adult life I also had not been fired.

Therapy .03

"Hi David, how are things?"

"Good Rae. How are you feeling today?"

"I'm good." *laughs*

"Did you save any lives today?"

laughs "No, no live-saving so far today. So tell me what's been going on? Last session you talked about that girl, I can't remember her name…the one you've been going on all those adventures with."

"Yes, Cassy. She's a wild one."

"So how are things going with you two?"

"They're OK, we're planning another adventure to see the smallest church in the world. It's somewhere near Syracuse. I'm just along for the ride."

"So she's the one making all the decisions."

"Yes in a nutshell."

"How have your symptoms been lately?"

"About the same, the trip to outpatient, what, my fourth one was difficult but my boss was really understanding and I feel good again and I'm back to work."

"It's so much easier when you get someone who treats their workers well. That's great, I was nervous for a while you really weren't doing well. The psychiatrist over there was in touch with me."

"Yeah, it was a good experience."

"So what else, oh yeah, so you've been taking all your meds. It looks like they upped your Zyprexa for the time being. How have you been responding, OK?"

"Yeah, it's a bit more sedation but you know me, I can take it."

"Ohhh…well, as long as it's working. You notice a difference?"

"Just my mood symptoms. I feel a little more stable. I actually take that extra 5mg during the day. It evens me out."

"I have patients who do that too. Some people really like it, it kinda, like you said, evens their mood out." *Rae begins being occupied with her computer screen.*

"I'm pretty even-keel."

"Good." *laughs*

"What do you want to talk about today?"

"I'm not sure."

I begin to feel the quaking and nervousness. I'm comfortable with Rae but intimacy in therapy leaves me vulnerable. It's too hard. I feel like jumping out of my skin.

"I've been having like a lot of anxiety, lately."

I pause. I look away. I'm suddenly afraid I'll lose the power of speech. I panic.

"You said you've been having a lot of anxiety. Do you know what's causing that?"

"I…"

I can't look at Rae. I begin to feel aggression. I shove it down and I know if I hold out sometimes I pass through this feeling.

"I'm just so frustrated all the time."

"Uh huh."

I feel terror that if I disclose how I'm feeling she'll think I need to go back to the hospital. Worse, I'll go psychotic and die and end up in a black space of nothingness.

"I'm just so, uhhhh…I don't want to live at home."

"Uh huh."

"I don't want to feel so frustrated."

It's an honest attempt at intimacy.

"David, do you think those feelings are related to something in particular? Like how you would imagine a scenario playing out where you didn't feel that way?"

"Well I know that my passivity over problems builds up frustration and boils over into depression. I just…I don't know how to approach it."

I want to show her that I know what I'm talking about and have a handle on it. I have to store these feelings, it can't come out. A bad report will kill me.

"I think you're very right to point out how that works, go on…"

"How do I seem Rae? Am I OK?"

"Yeah you seem alright, a little anxious. Why what's up?"

"OK."

I feel a little relieved but stay tense the rest of the session as always.

Session #88. Still one foot in and one foot out. It was an honest attempt at intimacy.

Arizona

In 2 months my friend Dan and I leave for Arizona to work on a ranch. And it is then now our point of departure…

The land was kiln-dry with rattlesnakes and cracked rocks scattered over raised mounds of yellow earth. That burnt-yellowish landscape that evokes human sweat and time. In its weathered dwellers' casual intonations you hear the tangles with raw rains, brazen sun, and tusked rodents; recounted with a slight humor. For 3 months Dan and I marinated as that snake in the whiskey jar. I saw a swath of night sky from the trailer-porch that spanned as wide as to give the impression you beheld eternity, strange, beautiful, right there, the same place where you point to describe the Big Dipper when it's just a finger pointing at the universe. My insomnia went on for months from its spiders which weave the weirdest dreams. Like I mentioned before, time fades from your senses except by checking the slow decay of fleshy-skin on cow skulls. They're nailed there to fence-posts but no longer bleed. Bulls stand 150 yards away and still cause a twinge of fear. Fires that play with the shadows of ashy brush combing for the eyes of lions.

Independence/3rd Episode

After my time at the ranch I flew home. I was confident from living on my own, renewed from living in a foreign land and generally full of swagger. My arrangement with myself to become self-reliant ruminated as the plane hit the tarmac of Rochester International. I did it. I got a new job, moved into an apartment with some friends and began a second life.

The city-life was loud. I felt stifled like a song blaring everywhere you walked, an ornery horn someone sat on that just wonks a flat note for months. I wasn't interested in engaging with clubs, coffee shops or gatherings like I'd previously thought. Instead it was constantly trying to get away from the city.

In the apartment that was empty a lot I listened to the music of Slipknot to cope each afternoon and evening. Comforted by Sarah's 12-season collection of *The Simpsons*, but something wasn't sitting right. I didn't want to be here, and I did want to be here. The problems with cigarettes, stress, and not being active in mental health treatment anymore would have been concerns if my blinders weren't on. I was having trouble breathing clearly and I tried every allergy medicine, quit smoking, and it turned out to be a prolonged anxiety-attack with shortness of breath I fought for 2 months.

My job was manager for a catering company. I was a sort of jack-of-all-trades man, but the pace became too fast and the messiness of the operation made me wish for stability. At this point in my recovery I still have a plethora of active and unresolved personal issues. Neuroticism is the build-up of unprocessed thoughts, feelings, and experiences in my view. If you're neurotic it will fuck with you til you get therapy. Alienating from therapy and constantly rushing around in a rusted barely-braking vehicle all day to different events isn't helping me.

I assumed staying sober and taking medication would be enough to avert a crisis. In a foolhardy way that notion made me forget the necessity of treatment. After 4 months working for a catering company in constant disarray I had a psychotic episode.

At my computer I access Google platform and begin my workday. I'm wearing shoes with no socks, and I notice it, but it doesn't matter. As soon as I focus at the screen I feel a sudden sensation building in my head. I squint and try to shove it down. It builds more.

No one is in the office. I get up and begin to pace. It's building and building around my head. It's tightening now. The intensity of it is raising my fucking anxiety. I know it's bad. If it passes the threshold I'll lose it. I recognize the sensation as psychosis as soon as it breaks through.

I run out of the building and throw myself against the wall gripping the sides of my head, reeling and disoriented. I register that I have Ativan in the car and struggle up, slam my hand into the glove-box, take the container out and down 3 pills. Still gripping my skull I'm panicked, disoriented, and terrified.

I think I should go to the hospital. I know I should, I'm barely conscious enough to think. I get in my car and I know I shouldn't drive, but I have no one but Grandma to help me right now. The Ativan kicks in. I'm still freakishly and absurdly impaired as I hit I-90. I try to focus on the road as my head swims. Shooting pains and bodily pains. I can't stop thinking about how bad things are going to be again. All I can feel is how long it's going to take to recover. I'm so shocked and pain is all throughout my body. It's another one, and I cannot believe it.

I lived with my grandmother spending most days on the couch watching Champions League soccer, my mind racing, hearing voices when the TV wasn't on, unable to breathe unrestricted from anxiety.

Hearing Voices

The most common experience that leads to auditory hallucinations for me is to be under tremendous prolonged stress. I usually hear a scramble of voices coming from outside of me. When I say "outside of me," just imagine a boombox in the corner of the room, and when you turn it on out comes voices of nonsense. That is what I hear except there's absolutely no source for the voices. Hearing voices is classified as Auditory Hallucinations. AH fit under the label of psychosis.

Normally when you have a psychotic episode it's a trip to the hospital. You would need immediate emergency care. I have no idea what possessed me, but as I told my cousin Becca, "You're a lot stronger than me, but I did take a psychotic episode to the face, that was pretty insane." I said that 3 years after the episode. It took 3 years until I reached a slight remission where that could be comical. That's coming from a person who makes being blind at Thanksgiving comical.

A description of the symptoms of psychosis is unnecessary. They were really so unique and terrifying I will not go into them. Perhaps I'll whet your curiosity by saying my thoughts were songs like a jukebox on shuffle every second I was awake for 9 months. I'll leave it there. In those 9 months I began to think what the fuck is happening to me. Inside I knew that suicide had a high probability of occurring because it had become actually very rational. I never felt that before. It was the morally right thing to do. I still believe that.

I had lost everything, again.
I lost my job, my apartment, my sanity.

As soon as I began to start over I got curb-stomped after 4 months.

Schizoaffective Disorder raises the weight on you to live each day prior to living each day. Mental illness is a precondition before the conditions of life. You have an illness to start with, now find food, shelter, and handle the stress. When you can't find food, shelter and relief from stress you regress, or end up hospitalized.

In my case I fell back on family. You would assume someone is ruminating on their failure. That's actually the last thing on my mind. I'm trying to see if I can survive with my symptoms. It wasn't supposed to be this way. I was supposed to spread my wings and soar.

And dammit, I failed. I just don't have time to think about failure.

My therapist panicked and was visibly unsettled at my description of the new symptoms. My psychiatrist gave me phone counsel daily and toyed with my antipsychotic dosages. It got rid of the auditory hallucinations but not the never-ending constant stream of noise in my head.

So I moved back in with Mom and Dad. In my situation without them and their unconditional love and support, I was just another madman on the curb with no social value and too bizarre to want to talk to. I think that is likely the fate left for me without living security and access to insurance for medication to fall back on.

My dad helped me to apply for Social Security Disability. After waiting 2 years I showed in front of the judge.

I am a person trying to maintain honor.

All my life my number one value has been fairness.

I stand before a judge as a beggar to collect, no more than that.

At the end I break down crying when it hit me right then, as the words left my mouth, when I said, "I am disabled." Oh my days.

I qualify as I am disabled. I'm not scheming the system, I'm exactly why SS exists in our society. I go back to work when my symptoms go into remission in a year. I can't let words like disabled define what I am. It's reality, but I've always subscribed to the idea that you do as much with the limitations you have as humanly possible, and to do that, you, to give that effort, can qualify your day as honorable. The measurement of your actions must be measured by you alone. Considered, only to yourself, as what qualifies as honorable to you. If indeed you have any sense of what honor is I suppose. We're dabbling in the place where limitations are real and so is honor.

I develop tinnitus around the time of my third psychotic episode. I wore headphones everywhere I went. In the house I moved between areas where strategically placed fans could neutralize the buzz. But the buzz was unbearable. I will not expand on this. Suffice to say, tinnitus is terrifying. I was quite sure I'd never hear silence again.

9 months. Every second of every day a song in my head and buzzing in my ears. Stupid pointless pain. After 9 months my jukebox-head went into remission. The symptoms abated, enough to think about social life and work. Astonishing. It took 2.5 weeks to even question the remission as real.

It shakes your faith to its foundation when you're tortured intensely. I wasn't ever going to be normal, I realized that; it was always going to be me finding an alternative route. The PTSD from psychotic episodes still affects me. It was a slow build-back of testing my limits of what I could handle safely. Hey, what are you going to do? You live once and there's always a choice to quit or keep placing your punches.

My diagnosis of Schizoaffective Disorder did show just how serious a diagnosis it was and what my limitations could be in those 9 months.

The setback from my psychotic episode took 3 years in order to regain comfort with living a normal life again. I'm not the same person anymore. More wear on the treads and weariness plays around me like violins of fear, worry, shrieking madness-toward-death.

Building a Life After 3rd Episode

"Hey, would you like some honey in your tea?"

"Yes! Thank you so much. It's kind of you to always ask me that."

"You're welcome." *Grins.*

"Hey, I was hoping I could get your number, maybe we'll hit a movie or do something fun?"

"Ummm. Sure, yeah."

"Cool, I got you."

I'm starting to twist up but I stay calm.

"It's………."

"Awesome. I'll get a hold of you sometime soon."

The twisting is tightening.

"I'll let ya get back to work now."

"Cya."

She goes back to making coffee.

Thinks, "I did it. Fucking A I did it."

NAMI

I joined NAMI ROC in 2017. The Rochester Office of The National Alliance on Mental Illness brought me in as a friend does a friend who's lost everything and might need 50 bucks and a place to stay for a few nights. Trained in 2 NAMI programs, Ending the Silence and In Our Own Voice, I began doing the Rochester school districts as a speaker, and for IOOV I went into treatment centers and various church events and community spaces. At first it was hard. I was squeamish, prone to reading off a paper copy of my story.

Kristina was instrumental in helping me and pushed me to improve as a speaker. There were growing pains, but I love that she held a standard up to me. K was always quick to support me when it was tough or I was down on myself. We had many diner breakfasts between class-periods to become great friends.

"Hey man, you kicked ass in there."

"I felt pretty good about it."

"You should, you were GREAT," K says.

"I was going to hit up a diner between classes, you wanna come with?" K says.

"Of course, let's go get fed."

"Alllright," K says to me.

At Diner.

"So, what's been going on man?"

K drops her voice into a shallower real tone.

"I feel like we're such good buddies now. When I see we're scheduled together I'm totttally stoked."

When she says "stoked," her head launches upward and on return down, her face beams.

"So…how have you been man? I haven't heard from you in a while."

"Pretty good. Been thinking about taking some classes at Writers and Books."

"Oh yeah, right on."

"Yeah, just to pass the time maybe work the craft a little, you know, little by little."

"You're so funny." K smiles.

The conversation continues in good nature with plenty of smiles until it's the next class period.

As I spoke more in the first year I made leaps in recovery. I gained self-esteem. I understood facts about my mental illness from treatment, but getting in a room of people and shepherding them out there helps deeply internalize them. Once I knew the facts from literally preaching the gospel, I gained the confidence to face anyone without shame. In the pharmacy I saw a quotable magnet that summed up my NAMI experience.

"Life begins at the end of your comfort zone."

I start with the effect it had on my life, but everything genuine and meaningful about being a public speaker centers on the mission. I'm not there for self-esteem, all I'm thinking about is reaching a room of teenagers who might know someone in need of help or who need to hear this themselves. To spread the message of suicide prevention and give stories of hope is the center, but I just couldn't help noticing changes in myself. What I noticed was

I was walking into a room of 100 kids with no preparation and going off-the-cuff riffing on the video presentation. I said 12 words in 4 months at Ruby Tuesday. I noticed that when someone asked me about my mental illness or how I was doing the answer was, "Sure." Before it was a blast of anxiety and shame. The biggest thing was that I started being conversant enough with people to start dating again.

"That movie was good. I dug it. That girl kind of reminds me of you: dark hair, young, obsessed with her dog."

"Is that all that reminds me of her?"

"Well, you know your winning personality sort of can't be incorporated on-screen. It's too big for Hollywood."

"Omg, stop it dude."

"Hey facts is facts."

"OK, yeezy."

A So-Called Life

Joelle, a family friend, reached out and invited me to hang a year into my NAMI work. I heard stories about her crossing states to strip and her insane relationship with alcohol so I was expecting a wildcard.

Joelle is very kind and also seductive in a way that doesn't make me uncomfortable. Little do I know Joelle is going to introduce me to many people; in fact, she will be the entryway into recovery circles.

It was difficult to build a social circle from scratch, and that a sober community was just where I belonged didn't make it easy. My previous social life was always frustrating without people to relate to my illness and alcoholism. There were nights driving home where bridges looked appetizing to slam a car through. Or woeful feelings of disconnection, wondering what more there is to plague and divide me against the recovery.

Had I known just how life-changing it would be, to share deep dark things you seal in your head, I would have realized I needed a community of people to share my secrets. Secrets are also another word for shame.

The walls of the dusk-light of Javas, a mood cafe, are adorned with paintings from perhaps artists that passed through colleges or scenes. In time the various pieces feel like home adornments. The curvy surreal lips of the cartoonesque brunette grinning acidly. Nicknames for paintings such as "The Layne Staley." Even vestibules and eastern statutes take on a feel of home.

When I am accepted by my peers the comfort is not there. The comfort in shame is no comfort. However to feel a fellowship among us there is a connection of how we are oriented. To put it plainly, Murphy's Law is down the street at the intersection of East and Alexander. The bar whose name suggests I can't just have a single drink which my bones now tell me. Can't be in those unfulfilling social circles without connection. Can't be around alcohol anymore. The fellowship is where what could go wrong is pacified by knowing what to do that's right, no mystery, it's in the circle, and to trip to Taco Bell at 2 AM oddly with friendly crazies becomes more of a feeling of wellness than 6 drinks and staring over a dance floor, who's going home with whom, you again watching, and when that elation drops as the shuffle to the door ensues, you stand amid friends with their girls and can't see yourself past the next weekend when you'll try the bar scene over once more. And that's about as good as it's going to get.

Confidence grew. I always added to conversations. I never subtracted. The community welcomed me, also known as the fellowship of AA. God, were there those nights of doubting myself though. Not knowing if I was acceptable and pounding the steering wheel on the drive home. There was something I wanted that I saw in those around me. Perhaps the free-speech uninhibited, uncontrolled, loose and fun. I always wanted that way of feeling I'd lost after my break. Also the free-speech that took things I thought too dark to say aloud, and made them everyday mannerisms met with a collective laughter. Never did I think suicidal thoughts could be all that funny. Wrong. Never did I think my wreckage of the past could be an, "Oh No, here it comes," and laughter; but not forgetting the compassion and genuine concern was there at every juncture.

I worked as an Uber Driver and NAMI speaker making enough money to get by living with my parents. Being an Uber Driver, people often remarked I was incredibly good at it as I'm nice and easy to talk to. It became my favorite job I'd ever had with total control of schedule and it put me in the city to drop by on friends gathering at Javas or visit Joelle or Kury at their homes.

There was much work to do in therapy to get me to a better place. To get that free-feeling, but I always felt 100% free with Kury as we are both abstract thinkers and I less capable but serviceable to converse with Kury, a savant of sorts.

Kury is my teacher and it's unnecessary to reference his lessons as they have permeated into my way of life. Suffice to say, in him I found total acceptance. With his total acceptance came my personality flooding the fuck out even when around others there was always a bind at times.

Confidence grew. NAMI offered self-esteem. My third psychotic break has gone into as much remission as could be expected. What was there to do? I took journalism classes at local colleges. I began experimenting with direction in my life. It was like my life and mental health were finally leveling out. I was going on dates again. At that time, I'm genuinely content with how things were going with my so-called life.

It wasn't perfect and to say so is disingenuous. The transformation was building through repeated steps of actions. The thrashing storm just let up a little and I walked on with a pace like it never touched me.

But there's work to be done.

Pandemic/Hardcore Therapy

This entire memoir could be summed up in one way. That way is, how I lost my mind, and how I got my mind back. This last section is the final piece and it's all about how I got my mind back.

The still ongoing pandemic I spent with family in total isolation. I had a lot of time alone. I started looking back at my past a lot.

There have been problems with cognitive impairments all through my 20's. My friend Kury had introduced me to some mantras and Eastern Philosophy, but my biggest problems lie in the amount of unprocessed experiences, thoughts and feelings I had stored up over 12 years. The issues I'd never faced and thus carried with me.

My conception of neurotic is a build-up of unresolved experiences, poisonous beliefs and feelings that press and fuck with you until you explore them in contemplation. The most important part is allowing yourself to feel whatever comes up. The last step is to see the *Truth*, not the "truth" I want either, self-deception, in other words, and to understand what this stuff meant to me.

Once I had created my own frame of reference for exploring I was off. There are dangers to doing therapy on yourself surely, but at the time I had to dig into these issues. It got dark, a lot. Very dark. I refused to look away from the dark. The truth of the dark too. The truth of the dark. That could kill you depending on what you are in your bones, and there is a very distinct way to understand truth and to feel its predominating certainty toward an issue. I fought to see the truth, the benefit of that is to know when someone says something about you, or you question yourself, just how much credence that has, and just how much bullshit they're talking. With enough time you do begin to think not many people are doing what you're doing, and that's frustrating because you begin to see how society will rip itself apart without those practices. Especially without truth of the dark.

Step by step, experience by experience in some cases: Shame, Sex Relations, Trauma, Aggression, Hostility, and more. I began unpacking them slowly on my own.

Painting about my issues to see them visually helped me in a completely different way to understand them. Painting for me is utilitarian. It's done as a benefit to further advance my understanding of myself in the world.

My method worked on Shame so I emailed my psychiatrist to say I was very ready to go all in on therapy. I work with Kristin and I've made more progress with her in 6 months than the previous 10 years in therapy. Why? Because I was ready to be intimate in therapy. I could trust my mind.

For periods of my life suicidal thoughts went on 50% of the day, for a year or so, and homicidal thoughts repeating in my head for a year. It's really hard to make sense of those experiences because they seem to indicate bad apple, or fucked-up personality. The hardest were the homicidal thoughts. I read the book *The Imp of the Mind*, a brave piece of literature that helped me understand those who feel guilt, shame and torn up by the thoughts and impulses are those that, for human purposes, are not the ones going to act on them. When I lessened the emotional reaction I had to them I was able to live with them. Then they became a lot less frequent.

When I looked for the truth in the dark, what I know as truth is that there's no such thing as absolute certainty. I know in myself how utterly preposterous those thoughts and impulses were to even act on them, and it always felt that way, except the repetitious nature leaves you fraught with worry. How could I think those things? Am I bad? Am I a serial killer? I asked every question no matter how dark, and I went as dark as the black sinks. In my method I pin questions into degrees of Yes or No. You must allow for total vulnerability to the question.

"Don't give me the answer I want. I don't want the answer I want. Don't tense. Don't interfere with it. Don't influence."

When you get to truth it's unmistakable. You can never mistake the *Truth*.

Now I know just what I am. I'm one of the good guys, always have been, but I do not dismiss the darkness as something we don't find in humans, period. In fact I certainly have a dark-side, I'm just a lot less dark in my nature than I hazard to say many people are. It took bravery and total vulnerability to get there, but I'm glad I did it. I'm just worried about people who **aren't** doing that and what that means now. It's no stretch to say, every human being needs truth of the dark.

A common misconception is that mentally ill people are violent–it's false–however, just look at society/human nature: it's a question any real person encounters. Although many of my intrusive thoughts amount to symptoms of my mental illness–what I found was a lot of beliefs about women that involved objectification and denying the reality of personhood of women.

This surprised me because I am very respectful of women and have been for my whole life. It scared me that relatively good people (I know I am one) can have these hateful beliefs. I even uncovered a trend in others, which is the point of my life, to find things authentically, not read and sponge them up, a former trend that was pathetic. I find pathetic is the most apt description for when men deny women equality out of insecurity.

I spent major amounts of time in self-examination to understand my beliefs toward women. I went back through every experience that I'd retained that ever needed to be looked at. I painted. I learned. I got to the truth of what I am. Nowadays, after all that work I can clearly understand where violence towards women comes from. Objectification, in crude terms, making someone over into an object, allows that object to be subjected to whims for it does not feel, think, or behave in a sentient way. This explains then the dislocation of them as a human with things like categorizing women by physical traits. It never fails to surprise me, men doing this regardless of age or occupation. Couple this with some men's fragile inferiority complex with women perceived as equal or superior, or take men's simple pains of relationship shortcomings, then the "I feel pain, so I blame women" model–these are only a few of the sick contents of men's minds leading to the perpetuation of sick ideas.

I see just how hard it's going to be for men to risk their integrity looking into the dark bravely to get better. When I say these are expressions of hatred, take into account men's objectification.

"Hate," a word that gets tossed around should never be brushed off. Hate is not just a catch-word in a cultural studies article. The contents of hate, when un-packed, will take a man to encounter vicious and terrifying things. I did the work and felt a lot of things. I see an uphill climb for men to be rehabilitated and women vindicated and I'm very pessimistic but try to stay hopeful.

That's one example of work I did in the pandemic. The most beautiful thing is nowadays I have my mind back. Without it you can't process things and thus you can't get at authentic truth.

As I worked through Shame I noticed feeling more space and creativity. As I worked through Hostility I got to a place where I have nothing to hide. That is a very powerful thing that you might not realize. When you have nothing to hide you're less inclined to feel hostile, because you're not at odds with anything about yourself, even while I object to my daily behavior all the time. I guess.

Perhaps I was just lucky to have been raised the way I am.

Along the way of the pandemic I came to the realization I had been institutionalized by the mental health system. While I survived for years on coping skills and assessing my symptoms every hour every day to survive, I have recently been getting away from those concepts on which I survived. I had to stop treating myself as a patient and like a person. I wake up every day excited to live now. That is astonishing. I left NAMI to not rely on any institution or organization to have any influence over how I define myself or where I derive worth from. I stand here today as what I am.

As much as I've recovered, each day presents new events. I became a crisis counselor in the beginning of 2021. I saw more extremes this world is producing especially in the young. As tired, excited, and weary as I am I still have one thing I hope to keep experiencing before death.

I'd like to continue to find the people who brush the evergreen needles with their hand. People in an upside down world who've seen and felt a lot and have journeyed a long ways to stand before me. You know them by their demeanor–it tells all. These people continually make the world bearable again.